100 PIECE1

MW00988887

8" QUILT BLOCKS

by
Marsha McCloskey

Contents

INTRODUCTION

My love of quiltmaking includes a fascination with geometric patterns. Like most quilters, I collect patchwork designs. Some I will use, others I will never find time for; but the pattern collection, the accumulation of ideas and possibilities is an important part of my quilting life.

In 1980, Sharon Yenter, owner of the quilt store, In the Beginning, asked me to do a Pattern of the Month for her shop. This was a pattern for a patchwork block or quilt that was given free to customers at the cash register. The pattern instructions and templates had to fit on one side of an 8 1/2" x 11" sheet of paper, so the designs were pretty simple. Eventually, those early designs became the basis for my first quilt pattern book, *Small Quilts*, which was published by That Patchwork Place in 1982.

In 1992, I am still producing a new design for the store each month. Most of the patterns over the twelve years have been for 8" pieced blocks, so when I decided to publish this collection of designs, there were many patterns from which to choose. Most, but not all of the patterns in this book have been in the Pattern of the Month series. A few new patterns were added where necessary to complete the page layouts and to replace Pattern of the Month designs that included curved seams or applique, which I decided not to include in this collection.

Choices also had to be made in planning this project about how much space to allow for block designs and how much to allow for instructions for cutting and sewing and for general quilt construction. Accepted wisdom in the quilt book publishing business tells us that every book must stand alone and give the reader every technique needed to produce the patterns presented. The truth is that most quiltmakers today have more than one quilt book and have access to classes, guilds, teachers and videos. I have written several technique books myself and don't feel a need to repeat all the same information here (though some basic cutting and piecing information is offered). In order to have the space to present all one hundred 8" pieced block patterns, I am trusting that the reader can find good basic quiltmaking instruction in a number of places. I heartily recommend my own books, of course, and a few others that a quilter would find helpful. Here is a list of just a few good "how to" books. They are available in most quilt shops and various mail order catalogs.

• *Lessons in Machine Piecing.* Marsha McCloskey. Bothell, WA: That Patchwork Place, Inc., 1990. Ten easy lessons take you painlessly from straight seams to curves on the sewing machine.

• *Guide to Rotary Cutting.* Marsha McCloskey. Seattle, WA: Feathered Star Productions, 1990. Ready reference for cutting accurate pieces for quilts without templates. Includes straight and bias-strip piecing.

• *How to Improve Your Quilting Stitch.* Ami Simms. Flint, MI: Mallery Press, 1987. The complete guide to making smaller, more even stitches by hand.

• *Heirloom Machine Quilting.* Harriet Hargrave. Lafayette, CA: C &T Publishing, 1990. The best guide to quilting with a sewing machine.

• *Happy Endings.* Mimi Deitrich. Bothell, WA: That Patchwork Place, Inc., 1987. Dozens of binding techniques for finishing the edges of your quilt.

ABOUT THE PATTERNS

An alphabetical Index of the names of the one hundred patterns is on page 8. The patterns begin on page 9. For your convenience, templates and instructions for the 8" blocks have been grouped in two-page layouts. Without turning a page, you will find all the needed drawings, templates and instructions to make your chosen block design.

For each 8" pieced block design, you will find the following:

• A shaded drawing indicating fabric value placement and how many fabrics to use.

• Cutting instructions are given in the form of a list of templates needed and how many to cut of each one. A "+" in the cutting instruction indicates a color change. (For example: "Cut 2 + 2" means cut two of one color fabric and two more of another.) An "R" in the cutting instruction means "reverse" and applies to pieces cut as mirror images or reversals. (For example: "Cut 1R1" means cut one shape with the template as it appears in the book and then turn the template over to cut one shape reversed.)

• A line drawing of the piecing order with

numbers indicating template placement.
• Numbered templates.

The templates are multi-use templates intended to fill the needs of as many quiltmakers as possible.
   • Each template has a number, which is referenced in the cutting instructions and piecing diagrams for the blocks.
   • The inner line is the sewing line; the outer line is the cutting line and includes the 1/4" seam allowance.
   • Triangle points have been left on to aid in measuring for rotary cutting, but lines show where to trim the points for easy matching.
   • A drawing of a rotary cutter means that the shapes can be easily cut with a rotary cutter and cutting rulers with standard dimensions.
   • Grain lines are for lengthwise or crosswise grain of the fabric and are shown with an arrow on each piece. Two arrows on a triangle mean that the same shape is used in some designs with the straight grain on the long side and in others with the straight grain on the short side. Straight grain should fall on the outside edge of the block or pieced unit.

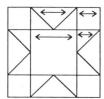 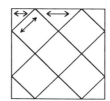

MAKING TEMPLATES

If you cut fabric with scissors, you will need a set of pattern pieces or templates to make each unit block design. Carefully trace the templates from the book onto graph paper or tracing paper. To make templates without seam allowances for traditional hand piecing techniques, trace on the inner, sewing line. For machine piecing where seam allowances are included, trace on the outer line of the templates. Trace accurately and transfer to your templates all the information printed on the templates in the book. Use removable tape to hold your tracing paper in place on the page as you work. Be precise. Make a template for each shape in the design.

Use paper templates to cut around with

scissors or in conjunction with a ruler and rotary cutter. Paper templates are simply cut out of the paper on which they are drawn.

Use stiffened templates to trace a pencil line on the fabric to guide your cutting. To make stiffened templates, roughly cut out paper pattern pieces outside of the cutting line. Glue each shape to a thin piece of plastic (X-ray film is ideal, lightweight poster board works, too). Cut out the paper pattern and its stiffening together.

Templates

ROTARY CUTTING

If you prefer no-template rotary cutting methods to the use of scissors and templates, carefully measure each template provided for cutting dimensions, and compare cut patches to the templates to check for accuracy. You can also use these dimensions for strip piecing squares, rectangles and triangles.

Some templates display a little drawing of a rotary cutter, a picture of the shape to cut and a cutting dimension. The cutting dimensions of these shapes will match the markings on standard cutting rulers and are recommended for cutting without templates.

Often, however, you will find the cutting dimensions of pattern pieces in this book do not correspond to markings on standard cutting rulers. Because of the drafting requirements of making all the blocks the same finished outside measurement, dimensions of individual pieces can be in various fractions, and I have elected not to give cutting dimensions for these templates. For these odd-size shapes, make an accurate paper template and tape it to the bottom of your cutting ruler with removable tape. You will then have the proper guide for cutting your shape.

Odd-size template
taped to ruler

Instructions are included here for four commonly used rotary cut shapes; squares, rectangles, half-square triangles, and quarter-square triangles. More detailed instructions for rotary cutting can be found in the *Guide to Rotary Cutting* booklet (see page 2).

To get started, you will need a rotary cutter with a fresh blade, a cutting mat and various cutting rulers.

Rulers for rotary cutting are 1/8" thick transparent acrylic and come in an array of sizes with a variety of markings. For the patterns in this book, the rulers most frequently used would be a 6" x 24" ruler marked in 1", 1/4", and 1/8" increments for cutting strips and an 8" Bias Square® ruler (a handy square marked in 1/8" increments with a 45° line running diagonally corner to corner).

When rotary cutting, hold the ruler down with the left hand (reverse these instructions if you are left handed), placing the smallest finger off the ruler to serve as an anchor and prevent slipping. Stand comfortably with your head and body centered on the cutting line. Hold the cutter in your right hand. Use a firm even pressure as you cut. Begin rolling the cutter before you reach the fabric edge and continue across. For safety, always roll the cutter away from you. The blade is very sharp, so be careful!

Cutting Straight Strips

The rotary method of cutting squares, rectangles, and other fabric shapes begins with cutting strips of fabric. These strips are then subcut to proper dimensions and angles. Strips of fabric are also used for borders: shorter ones are used for lattices, and long narrow strips are used in some design blocks. Strips can be cut from either the lengthwise or crosswise grain of the fabric.

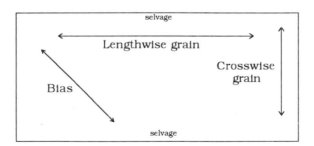

To cut strips:

1. Fold and press the fabric aligning the cross and lengthwise grains as best you can. Place fabric on the rotary cutting mat with the folded edge closest to your body. Align the Bias Square® ruler with the fold of the fabric and place a cutting ruler to the left.

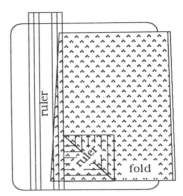

2. Remove the Bias Square® ruler and make a rotary cut along the right side of the ruler.

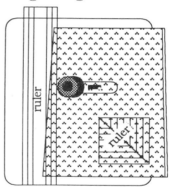

3. Cut strips of fabric the desired width as shown. Fabric can be folded again so that you will be cutting four layers at a time. Open fabric periodically to make sure you are making straight cuts. If fabric strips are not straight, use Bias Square® ruler to realign as in step #2.

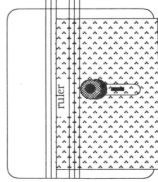

Squares and Rectangles

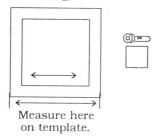

Measure here
on template.

1. First cut fabric in strips the measurement of the square including the seam allowance.
2. Using the Bias Square® ruler, cut the fabric into squares the width of the strip.
3. Cut rectangles in the same manner, first cutting strips the width of the rectangle including seam allowances, then cutting to the proper length. Check cut shapes against the templates to make sure they are the right size.

Half-Square Triangles

Two half-square triangles result when a square is cut in half on the diagonal. Straight grain is on the short sides and the bias on the long side .

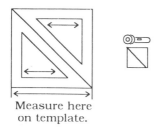

Measure here
on template.

To cut half-square triangles:
1. Cut a square the finished measurement of the short side of the triangle template, corner to tip including seam allowances.
2. Cut square diagonally corner to corner. Check the cut triangles against the template to make sure they are the right size.

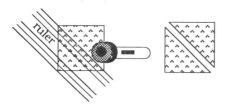

Quarter-Square Triangles

Four quarter-square triangles result when a square is cut in quarters on the diagonal. Straight grain is on the long side and the bias is on the short sides.

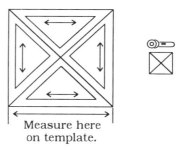

Measure here
on template.

To cut quarter-square triangles:
1. Cut a square the finished measurement of the long side of the triangle template, tip to tip including seam allowances.
2. Cut the square diagonally, corner to corner. Without moving the resulting triangles, line up the cutting ruler and make another diagonal cut in the opposite direction. Check the cut triangles against the template to make sure they are the right size.

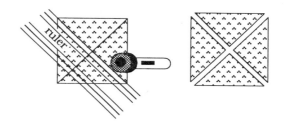

GENERAL RULES FOR MACHINE PIECING

1. Use 100% cotton white or neutral thread as light as the lightest fabric in the project. Use dark neutral thread for piecing dark solids.

2. Set the stitch length at 10-12 stitches per inch.

3. Sew 1/4" seams. Rotary cut pieces are generally slightly smaller than scissor cut pieces and, I find, require a scant (by two threads or so) 1/4" seam allowance for the most accurate results. Experiment with your

seam allowance until you find the measurement that yields the most accurate results.

4. Clip threads as you go. Make it a habit.

5. For most piecing, sew from cut edge to cut edge. Backtack if you wish, but when a seam line will be crossed and held by another, it is not necessary. When sewing set-in seams, however, it is necessary to backtack at the 1/4" seam line, as that seam will not be crossed by another.

6. Use chain piecing whenever possible to save time and thread. To chain piece, sew one seam, but do not lift the presser foot. Do not take the piece out of the sewing machine and do not cut the thread. Instead, set up the next seam to be sewn and stitch as you did the first. There will be a little twist of thread between the two pieces. Sew all the seams you can at one time in this way, then remove the 'chain'. Clip the threads between units.

7. To piece a unit block, sew the smallest pieces together first to form units. Join smaller units to form larger ones until the block is complete. (See piecing sequence illustration with each design block.)

8. Pin seams before stitching if matching is involved or if your seams are longer than 4". Pin points of matching first, then pin the rest of the seam, easing if necessary Keep pins away from seam lines, as sewing over them tends to damage the needle.

9. Press seams to one side, toward the darker fabric whenever possible. It is easier to press to one side and it puts seam-line stress on fabric instead of stitches. Pressing toward the dark prevents a shadow line of the darker fabric from showing through the lighter.

The two main exceptions are when seams are pressed open to distribute bulk like the middle of a pinwheel where eight points come together, and when, for matching purposes, seams are pressed in opposite directions, regardless of which is the darker fabric.

For patchwork, I press gently with a dry iron that has a shot of steam when needed. Take care not to overpress as it can stretch and distort fabric pieces, as well as make the fabric shiny where there are bumps.

Matching

The following matching techniques can be helpful in many different piecing situations:

1. Opposing Seams. Press seam allowances in opposite directions on seams that need to match. The two "opposing" seams will hold each other in place and evenly distribute the bulk.

2. Positioning Pin. A pin, carefully pushed straight through two points that need to match, and pulled tight, will establish the proper point of matching. Pin the seam normally and remove the positioning pin before stitching.

 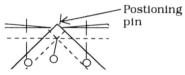

Postioning pin

3. The X. When triangles are pieced, stitches will form an X at the next seam line. Stitch through the center of the X to make sure the points on the sewn triangles will not be chopped off.

 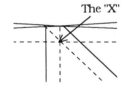

The "X"

4. Easing. When two pieces to be sewn together are supposed to match but instead are slightly different lengths, pin the points of matching and stitch with the shorter piece on top. The feed dog eases the fullness of the bottom piece.

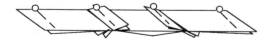

5. Set-in Seams. Where three seam lines come together at an angle, stop all stitching at the 1/4" seam line and backtack (you can mark the spot lightly with a pencil on the wrong side of the fabric). As each seam is finished, take the work out of the machine, position the next seam, and stitch in the new direction.

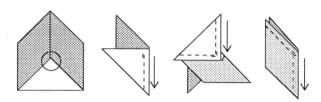

More detailed instruction in machine piecing techniques can be found in *Lessons in Machine Piecing* (see page 2).

FABRIC SELECTION

Choose 100% cotton fabrics that are preshrunk and tested for color. Study the shaded sketch provided with each 8" block pattern to give an idea of how many colors will be needed. The drawing shows one way the design could be interpreted. To try other value arrangements, trace the outline of the block and its shapes onto a piece of tracing paper and make your own shadings.

Decide which parts of the design will be the light, medium and dark values and assign each a color definition. For example the dark could be teal; the medium, rust; and the light, ecru with peach tones.

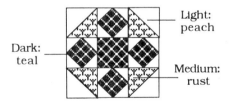

Contrast in value, color, and visual texture makes pieced designs visible. Visual texture is the way a print looks--is it spotty, smooth, plain, dappled, linear, rhythmical, or swirly? Are the figures far apart or close together? Mix large prints with small prints, flowery allover designs with linear rhythmical prints. Too many similar prints may create a dull surface or one that is visually confusing.

PATTERN NAMES AND ORIGINS

On the next page is a list of the patterns given in this book. Most are considered "traditional" and are found in several early sources of patchwork patterns such as the Ladies Art Company Catalog (1898-1930s), Ruth Finely's *Old Patchwork Quilts* (1929), Ruby McKim's *101 Patchwork Patterns* (1931), and Carrie Hall and Rose Kretsinger's *The Romance of the Patchwork Quilt in America* (1935). I have relied heavily on Barbara Brackman's research in her *An Encyclopedia of Pieced Quilt Patterns* to help with correctly identifying pattern origins. (Brackman is in parenthesis after citations that came directly from her book.) Because of space limitations, I have given only one source, and most times only one name for each pattern even though each could have several different names and have appeared in several different sources. For other blocks, if the designer is known, credit is given. Many of the blocks I designed and named: these are also noted.

Bibliography of
Quilt Block Design Sources

Brackman, Barbara, compiler. *An Encyclopedia of Pieced Quilt Patterns.* Lawrence, Kansas: Prairie Flower Publishing, 1984. Index of published quilt patterns before 1980.

Central Oklahoma Quilters Guild. *Ultimate Illustrated Index to the Kansas City Star Quilt Pattern Collection.* Oklahoma City, OK, 1990.

Finley, Ruth. *Old Patchwork Quilts and the Women Who Made Them.* Charles J.B. Lippincott: Philadelphia, PA, 1929.

Hall, Carrie A. and Rose G. Kretsinger. *The Romance of the Patchwork Quilt in America.* New York, NY: Bonanza Books, 1935.

Martin, Judy. *Ultimate Book of Quilt Block Patterns.* Denver, CO: Crosley-Griffith Publishing, 1988. This book contains 174 pieced block patterns, 139 designed by the author.

Martin, Judy. *Patchworkbook.* New York, NY: Charles Scribner's Sons, 1983. Dover edition, 1993. How to design original blocks and quilts.

McKim, Ruby Short. *101 Patchwork Patterns.* New York, NY: originally published in 1931, Dover edition, 1962.

INDEX OF PIECED 8" QUILT BLOCK DESIGNS

NOTES:

1. POM means Pattern of the Month.

2. aka means "also known as"

° *Plastic Templates*

BLOCK PATTERNS AND TEMPLATES

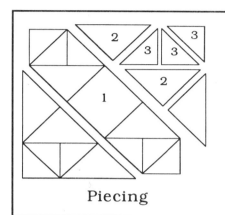

Castles in Spain

For one block:

Template **#1**: Cut 1
Template **#2**: Cut 4 + 4
Template **#3**: Cut 4 + 4 + 4

Piecing

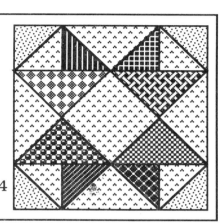

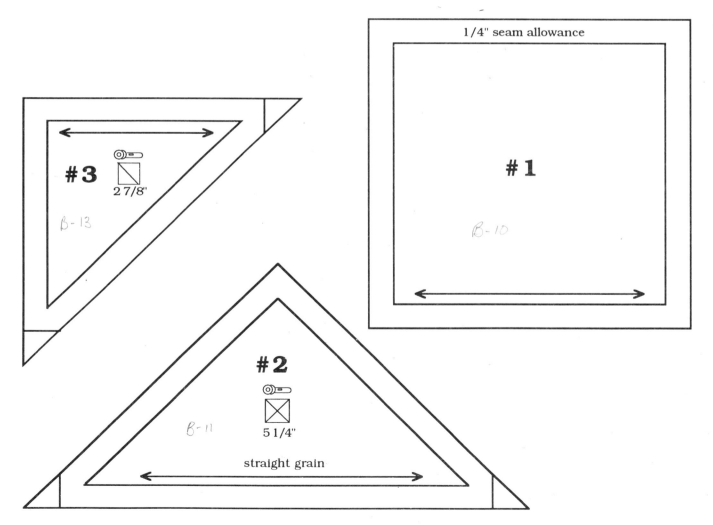

1/4" seam allowance

#1

B-10

#3

2 7/8"

B-13

#2

5 1/4"

straight grain

B-11

Rising Star

For one block:
Template **#1**: Cut 1 + 4
Template **#2**: Cut 8
Template **#3**: Cut 4
Template **#4**: Cut 4
Template **#5**: Cut 8
Template **#6**: Cut 4

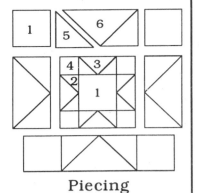

Piecing

Jack in the Pulpit

For one block:
Template **#1**: Cut 1
Template **#3**: Cut 4
Template **#5**: Cut 4 + 12
Template **#7**: Cut 4
Template **#8**: Cut 4

Piecing

Jack in the Pulpit

#1 & #3 same color
#7 & #8 same color
#5 all different

B-13

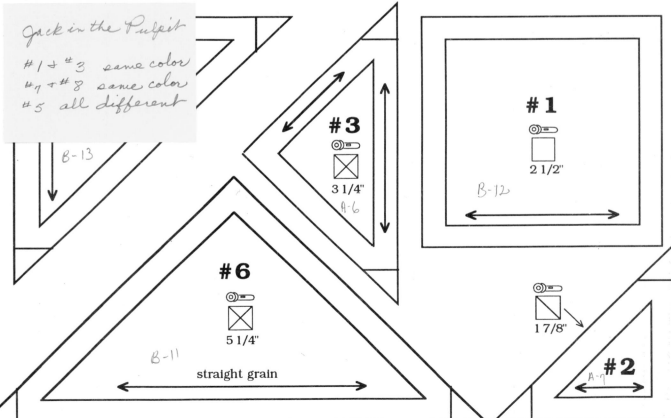

#3
3 1/4"
A-6

#1
2 1/2"
B-12

#6
5 1/4"
B-11
straight grain

#2
1 7/8"
A-7

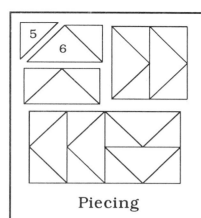

Dutchman's Puzzle

For one block:

Template **#5**: Cut 16
Template **#6**: Cut 8

Piecing

Dutchman's
Puzzle
#5 + #6 in 4 sq
4 colors

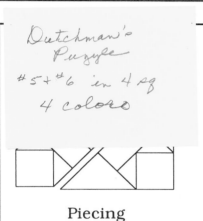

Piecing

Centennial

For one block:

Template **#1**: Cut 4
Template **#3**: Cut 8
Template **#6**: Cut 4
Template **#7**: Cut 4
Template **#9**: Cut 1

1/4" seam allowance

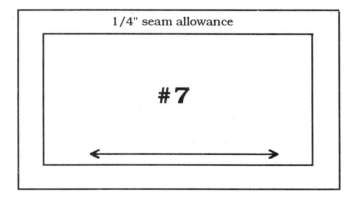

#7

#9

B-10

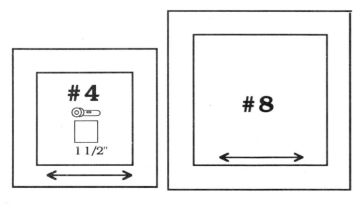

#4

1 1/2"

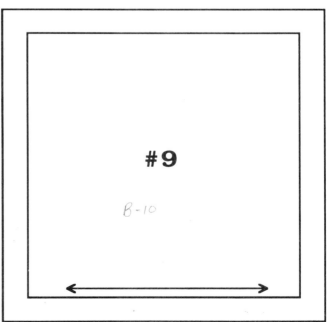

#8

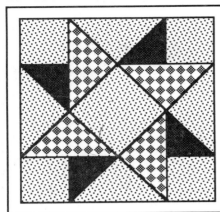

Judy's Star

For one block:

Template **#1**: Cut 1
Template **#2**: Cut 4 + 4
Template **#3**: Cut 4
Template **#5**: Cut 4

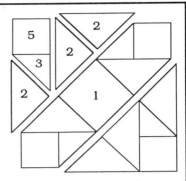

Piecing

Rambler

For one block:

Template **#1**: Cut 1
Template **#2**: Cut 4
Template **#3**: Cut 12
Template **#4**: Cut 16

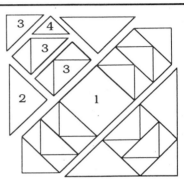

Piecing

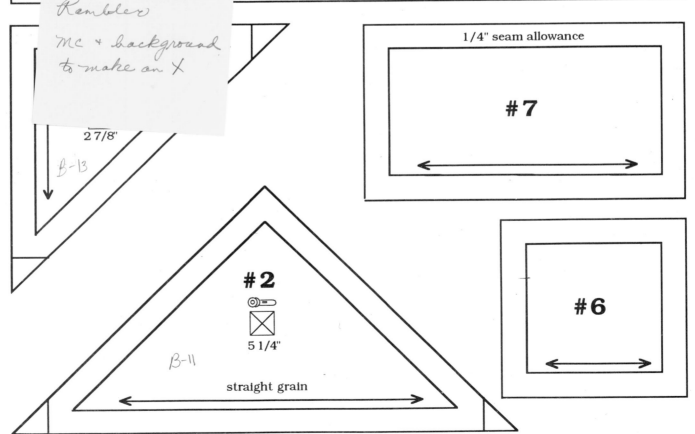

Rambler

mc + background
to make an X

2 7/8"

B-13

#2

5 1/4"

B-11

straight grain

1/4" seam allowance

#7

#6

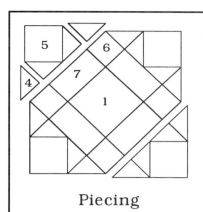

Piecing

Beacon Lights

For one block:

Template **#1**: Cut 1
Template **#4**: Cut 8 + 8
Template **#5**: Cut 4
Template **#6**: Cut 4
Template **#7**: Cut 4

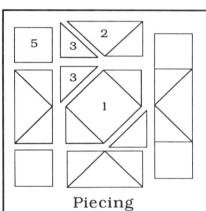

Piecing

Variable Star

For one block:

Template **#1**: Cut 1
Template **#2**: Cut 4
Template **#3**: Cut 8 + 4
Template **#5**: Cut 4

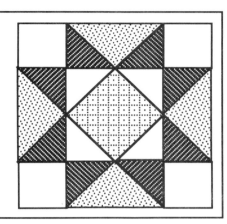

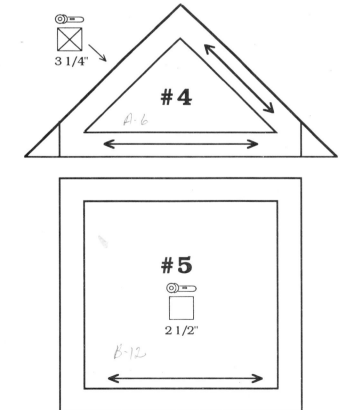

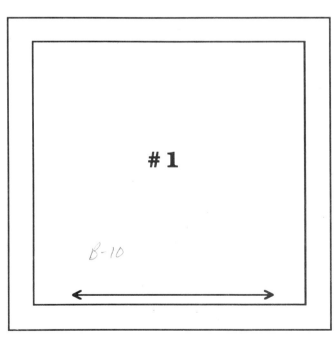

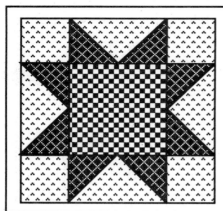

Sawtooth Star

For one block:

Template **#1**: Cut 1
Template **#2**: Cut 4
Template **#3**: Cut 4
Template **#4**: Cut 8

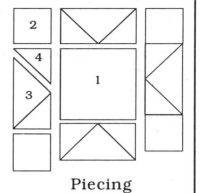

Piecing

King's Crown

For one block:

Template **#1**: Cut 1
Template **#2**: Cut 4
Template **#3**: Cut 4
Template **#4**: Cut 8

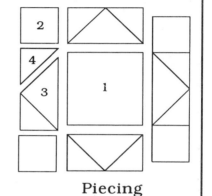

Piecing

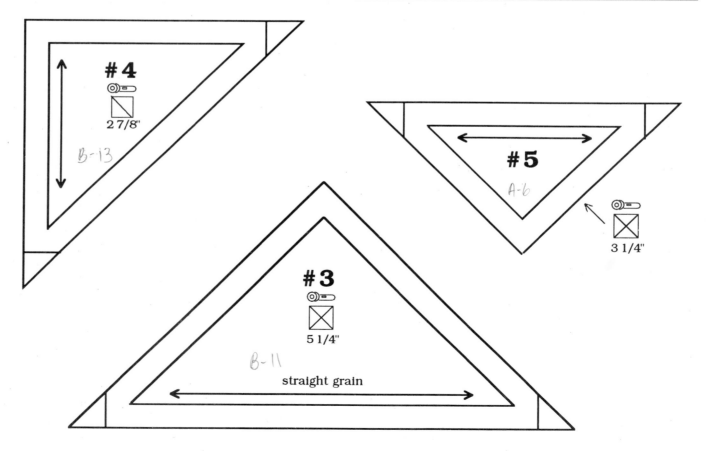

#4

2 7/8"

B-13

#5

A-6

3 1/4"

#3

5 1/4"

B-11

straight grain

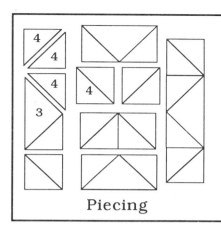

Star Puzzle

For one block:

Template **#3**: Cut 4
Template **#4**: Cut 8 + 8 + 8

Piecing

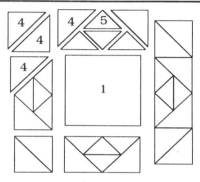

Grandmother's Favorite

For one block:

Template **#1**: Cut 1
Template **#4**: Cut 4 + 12
Template **#5**: Cut 4 + 12

Piecing

Grandmother's Favorite

Color as Russian the Corner

1/4" seam a

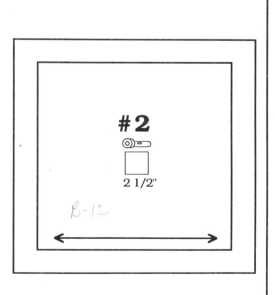

#2

2 1/2"

B-12

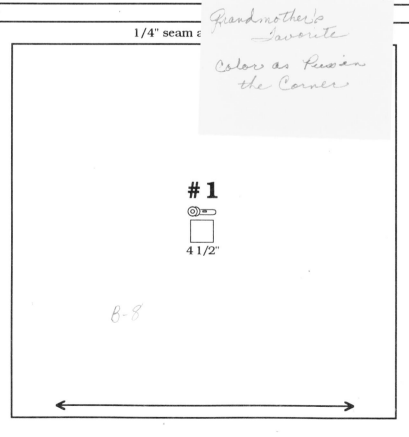

#1

4 1/2"

B-8

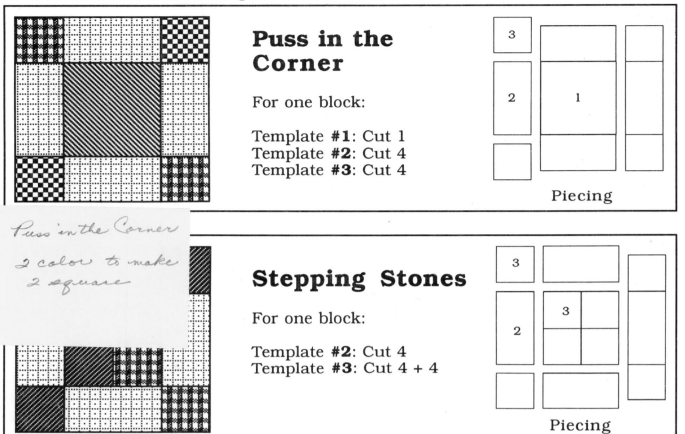

Puss in the Corner

For one block:

Template **#1**: Cut 1
Template **#2**: Cut 4
Template **#3**: Cut 4

Piecing

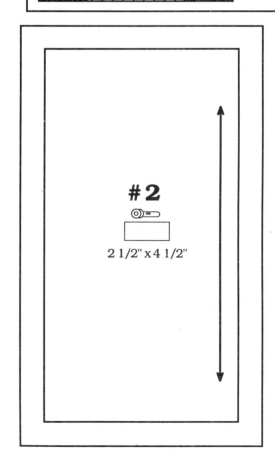

Puss in the Corner

2 color to make

2 square

Stepping Stones

For one block:

Template **#2**: Cut 4
Template **#3**: Cut 4 + 4

Piecing

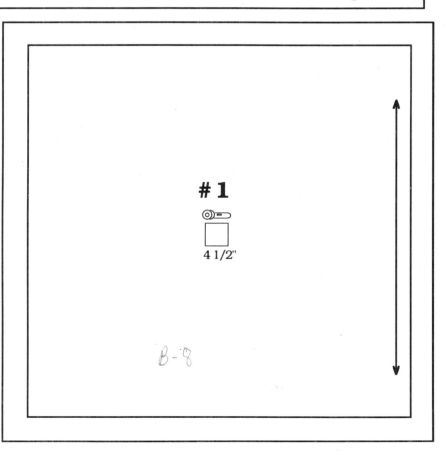

#2

2 1/2" x 4 1/2"

#1

4 1/2"

B-8

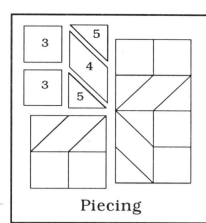

Piecing

Clay's Choice

For one block:

Template **#3**: Cut 4 + 4
Template **#4**: Cut 4
Template **#5**: Cut 8

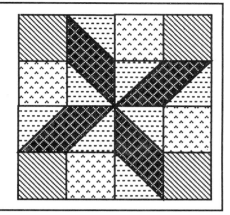

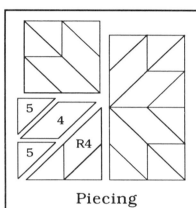

Piecing

Windmill Star

For one block:

Template **#4**: Cut 4 + R4
Template **#5**: Cut 8 + 8

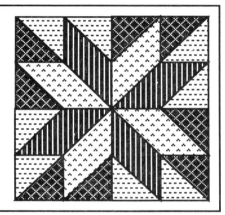

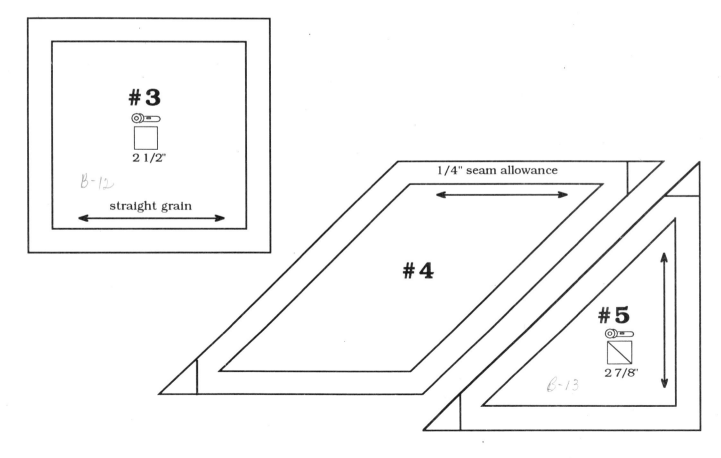

#3

2 1/2"

B-12

straight grain

1/4" seam allowance

#4

#5

2 7/8"

B-13

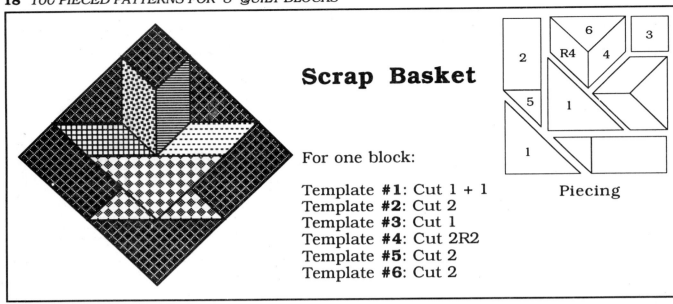

Scrap Basket

For one block:

Template **#1**: Cut 1 + 1
Template **#2**: Cut 2
Template **#3**: Cut 1
Template **#4**: Cut 2R2
Template **#5**: Cut 2
Template **#6**: Cut 2

Piecing

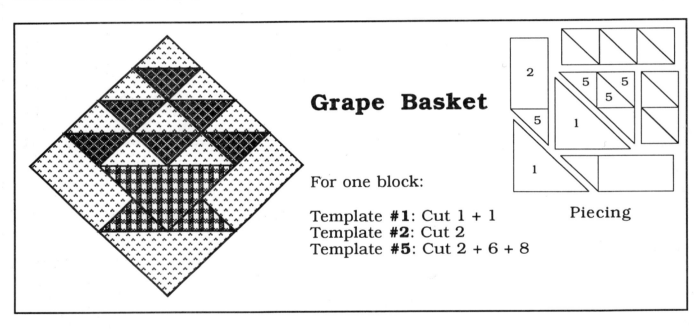

Grape Basket

For one block:

Template **#1**: Cut 1 + 1
Template **#2**: Cut 2
Template **#5**: Cut 2 + 6 + 8

Piecing

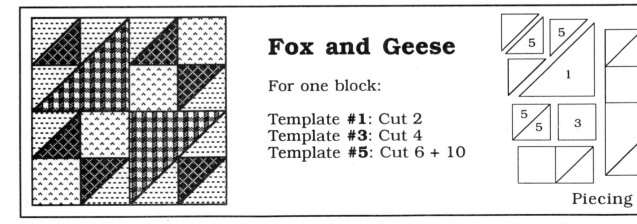

Fox and Geese

For one block:

Template **#1**: Cut 2
Template **#3**: Cut 4
Template **#5**: Cut 6 + 10

Piecing

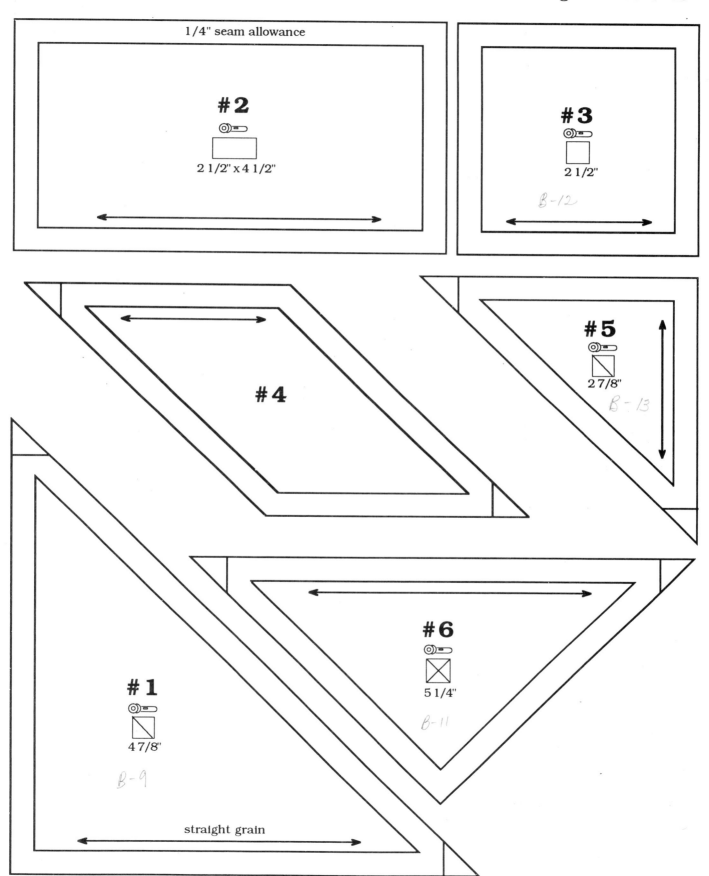

1/4" seam allowance

#2

2 1/2" x 4 1/2"

#3

2 1/2"

B-12

#4

#5

2 7/8"

B-13

#6

5 1/4"

B-11

#1

4 7/8"

B-9

straight grain

Ocean Waves

For one block:

Template **#1**: Cut 1 + 1
Template **#2**: Cut 12 + 12

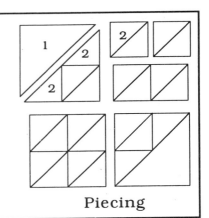

Piecing

Birds in the Air

For one block:

Template **#1**: Cut 4
Template **#2**: Cut 4 + 12

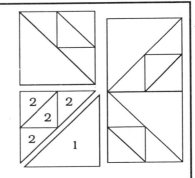

Piecing

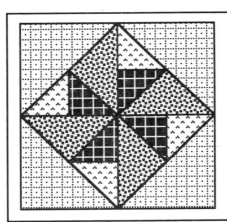

Flying Pinwheel

For one block:

Template **#1**: Cut 4
Template **#2**: Cut 4 + 4
Template **#3**: Cut 4

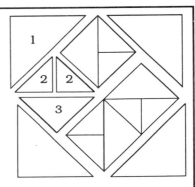

Piecing

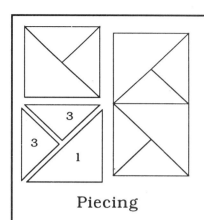

Piecing

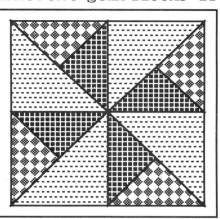

Whirligig

For one block:

Template **#1**: Cut 4
Template **#3**: Cut 4 + 4

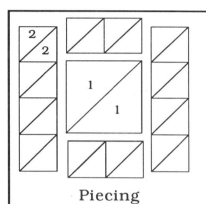

Piecing

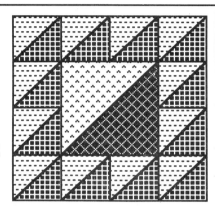

Lost Ships

For one block:

Template **#1**: Cut 1 + 1
Template **#2**: Cut 12 + 12

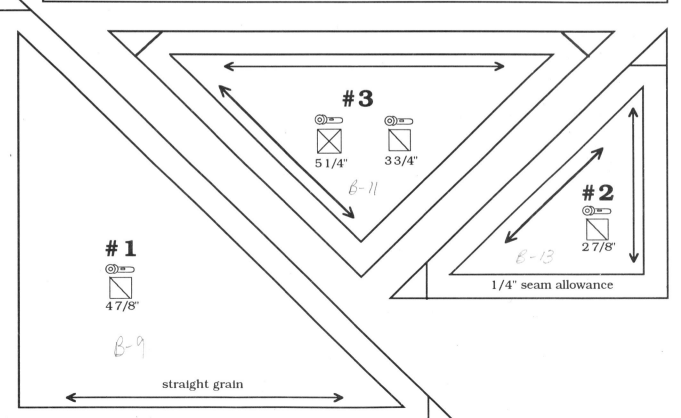

#3

5 1/4"   3 3/4"

B-11

#2

2 7/8"

B-13

1/4" seam allowance

#1

4 7/8"

B-9

straight grain

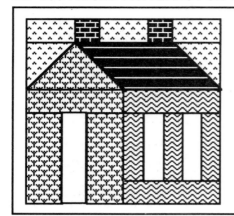

School House

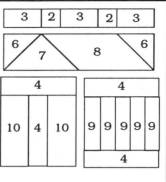

For one block:
Template **#2**: Cut 2
Template **#3**: Cut 3
Template **#4**: Cut 2 + 1 + 1
Template **#6**: Cut 2
Template **#7**: Cut 1
Template **#8**: Cut 1
Template **#9**: Cut 2 + 3
Template **#10**: Cut 2

Piecing

Chimneys and Cornerstones

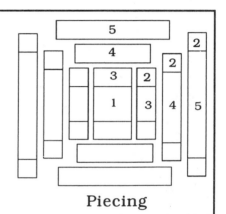

For one block:

Template **#1**: Cut 1
Template **#2**: Cut 12
Template **#3**: Cut 4
Template **#4**: Cut 4
Template **#5**: Cut 4

Piecing

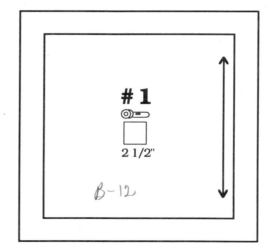

#1
2 1/2"
B-12

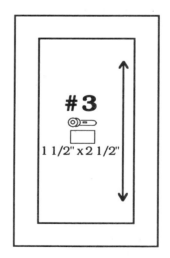

#3
1 1/2" x 2 1/2"

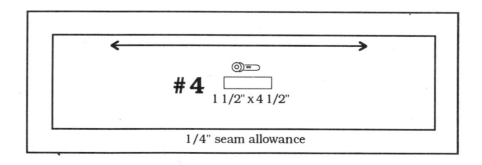

#4
1 1/2" x 4 1/2"

1/4" seam allowance

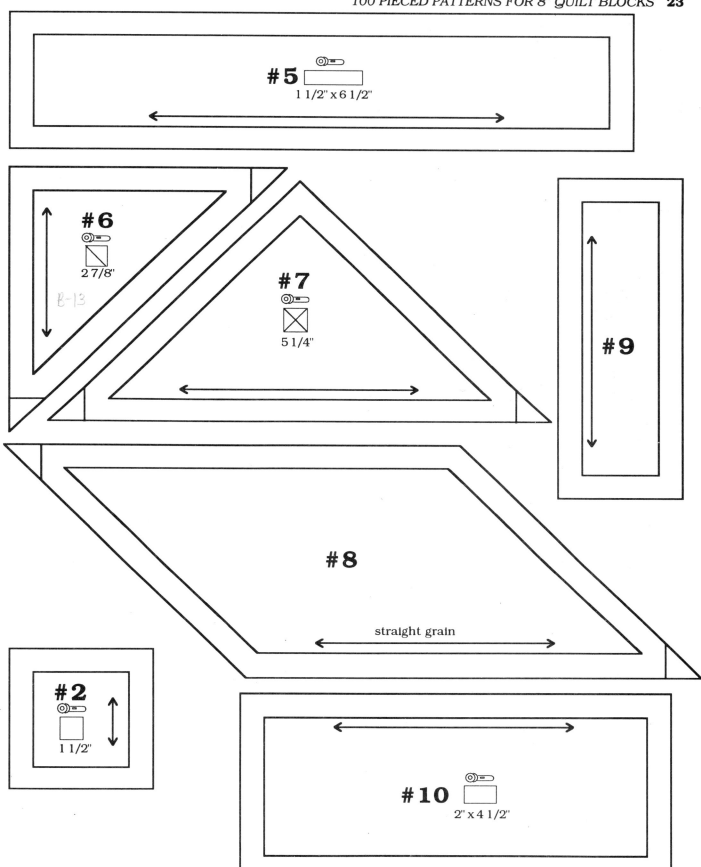

#5
1 1/2" x 6 1/2"

#6
2 7/8"
B-13

#7
5 1/4"

#9

#8
straight grain

#2
1 1/2"

#10
2" x 4 1/2"

Star Dreams Through Attic Windows

For one block:
Template **#1**: Cut 1
Template **#2**: Cut 8
Template **#3**: Cut 4
Template **#4**: Cut 4
Template **#5**: Cut 1 + R1

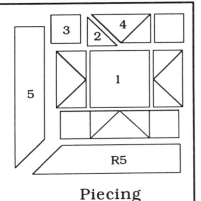

Piecing

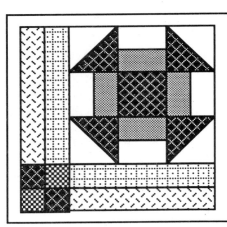

Log Cabin Quail's Nest

For one block:
Template **#6**: Cut 1
Template **#7**: Cut 4 + 4
Template **#8**: Cut 4 + 4
Template **#9**: Cut 2 + 2
Template **#10**: Cut 2 + 2

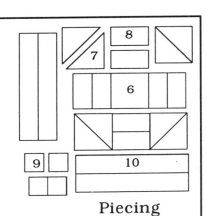

Piecing

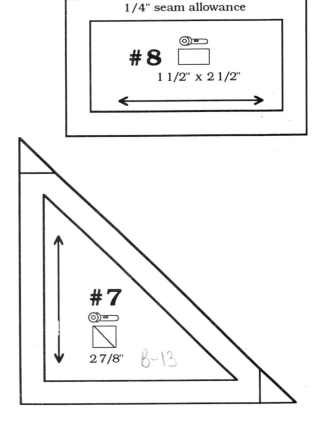

1/4" seam allowance

#8

1 1/2" x 2 1/2"

#7

2 7/8" B-13

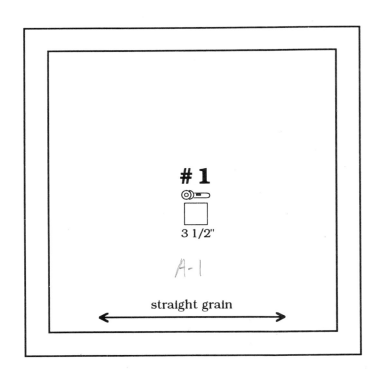

#1

3 1/2"

A-1

straight grain

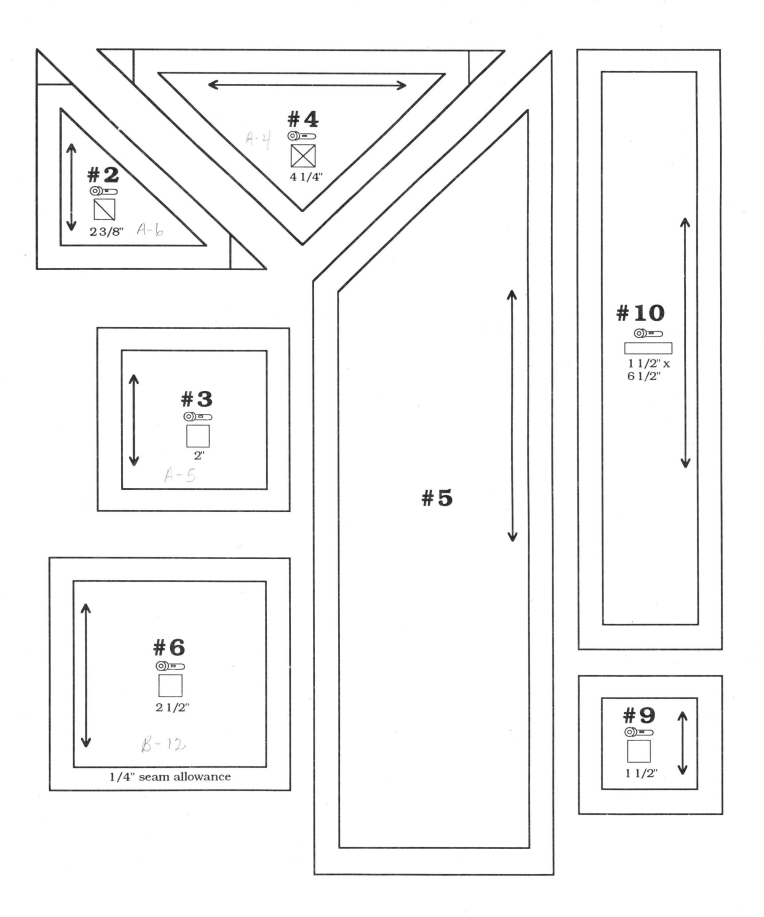

#4

A-4

4 1/4"

#2

2 3/8"   A-b

#3

2"

A-5

#10

1 1/2" x
6 1/2"

#5

#6

2 1/2"

B-12

1/4" seam allowance

#9

1 1/2"

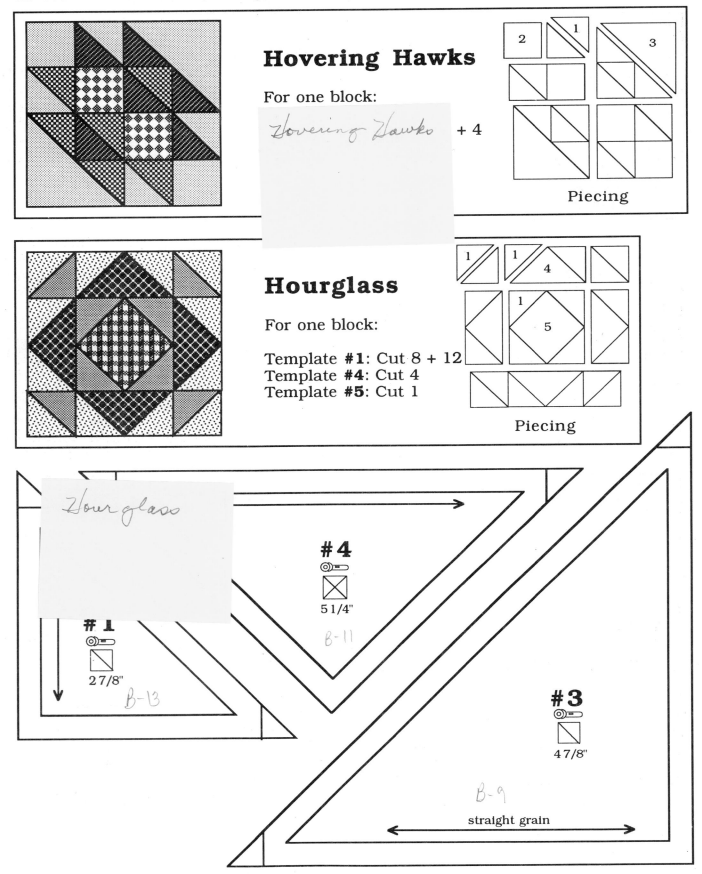

Hovering Hawks

For one block:

Hovering Hawks   + 4

Piecing

Hourglass

For one block:

Template **#1**: Cut 8 + 12
Template **#4**: Cut 4
Template **#5**: Cut 1

Piecing

Hourglass

#4

5 1/4"

B-11

#1

2 7/8"

B-13

#3

4 7/8"

B-9

straight grain

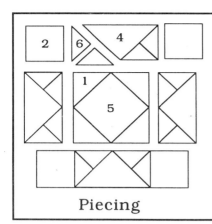

Missouri Star

For one block:

Template **#1**: Cut 4
Template **#2**: Cut 4
Template **#4**: Cut 4
Template **#5**: Cut 1
Template **#6**: Cut 8 + 8

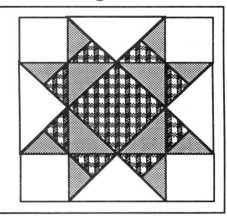

Piecing

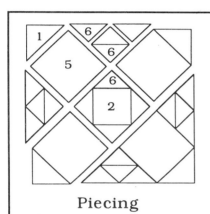

Mosaic

Mosaic
2 colors to make
an X

+ 16

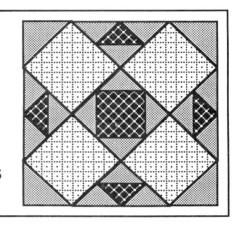

Piecing

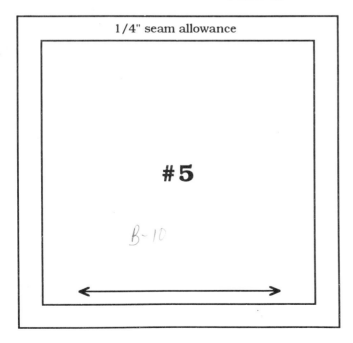

1/4" seam allowance

#5

B-10

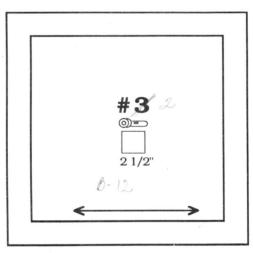

#3 *2*

2 1/2"

B-12

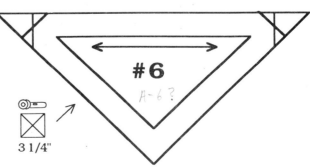

#6

A-6 ?

3 1/4"

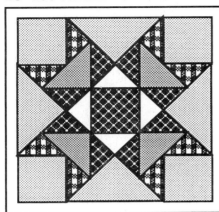

Broken Star

For one block:

Template **#1**: Cut 4
Template **#3**: Cut 1 + 4
Template **#4**: Cut 4
Template **#6**: Cut 4 + 8 + 8

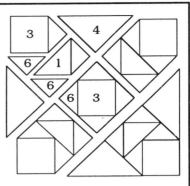

Piecing

Rosette

Rosette
5 colors to
make sq in a
square

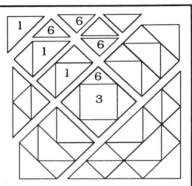

Piecing

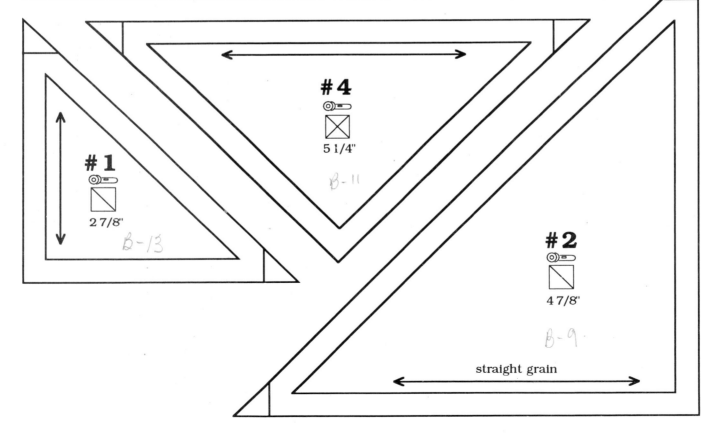

#4
5 1/4"
B-11

#1
2 7/8"
B-13

#2
4 7/8'
B-9

straight grain

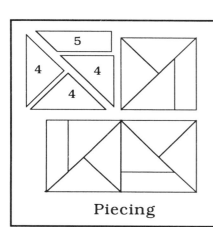

Pinwheel

For one block:

Template **#4**: Cut 8 + 4
Template **#5**: Cut 4

Piecing

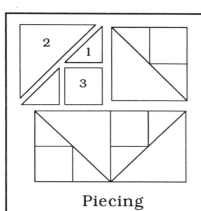

Review

For one block:

Template **#1**: Cut 4 + 4
Template **#2**: Cut 2 + 2
Template **#3**: Cut 2 + 2

Piecing

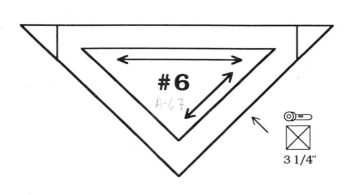

#6

A-67

3 1/4"

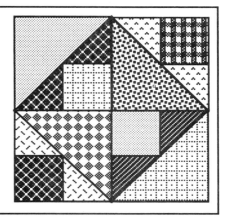

1/4" seam allowance

#3

2 1/2"

B-12

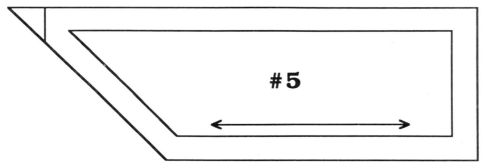

#5

Star Tile

For one block:

Template **#1**: Cut 8 + 4 + 4
Template **#2**: Cut 4
Template **#3**: Cut 4
Template **#4**: Cut 4
Template **#5**: Cut 1

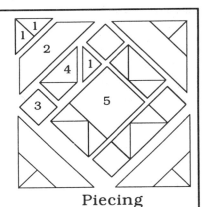

Piecing

Pinwheel Mosaic

For one block:

Template **#2**: Cut 4
Template **#4**: Cut 4+4+4
Template **#6**: Cut 4

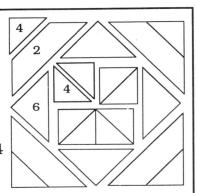

Piecing

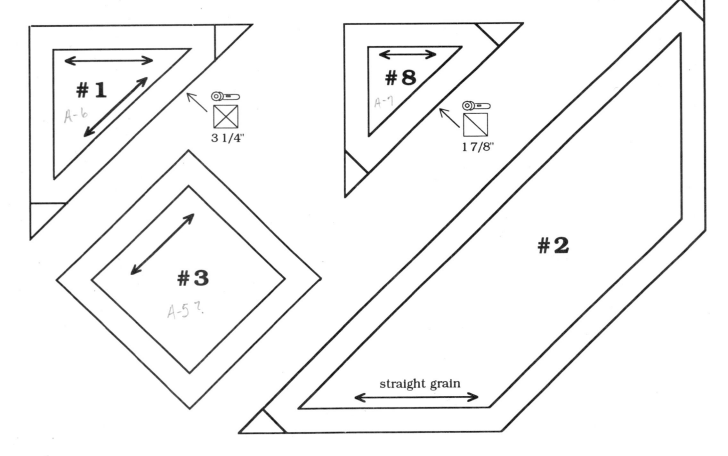

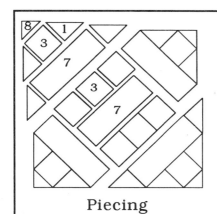

Piecing

Friendship Chain

For one block:

Template **#1**: Cut 12
Template **#3**: Cut 8 + 2
Template **#7**: Cut 4 + 1
Template **#8**: Cut 4

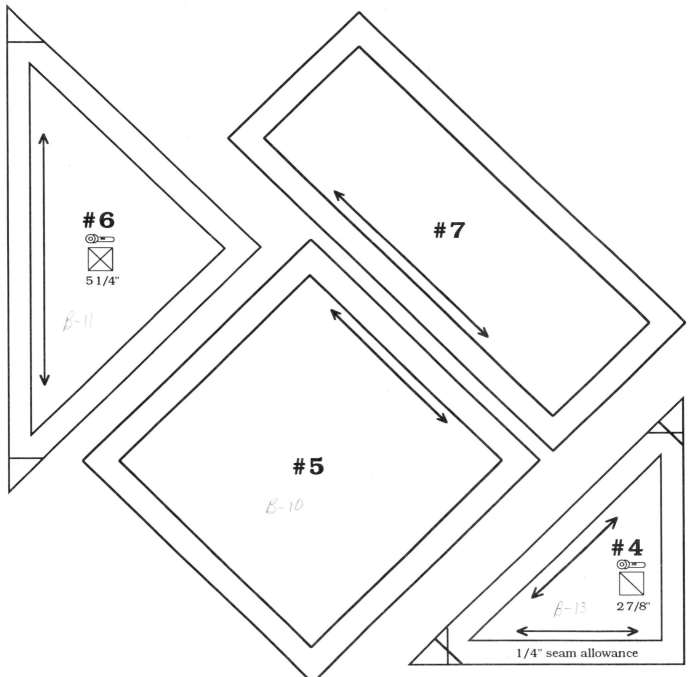

#6

5 1/4"

B-11

#7

#5

B-10

#4

2 7/8"

B-13

1/4" seam allowance

Key West Beauty

For one block:

Template **#1**: Cut 4
Template **#2**: Cut 8
Template **#3**: Cut 4
Template **#4**: Cut 4

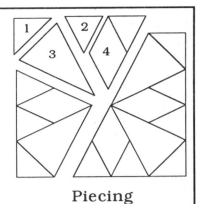

Piecing

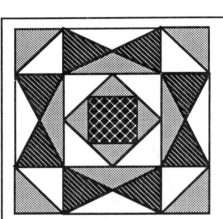

Ish River Rose

For one block:

Template **#1**: Cut 4 + 8
Template **#2**: Cut 8
Template **#5**: Cut 1
Template **#6**: Cut 4
Template **#7**: Cut 4 + 4

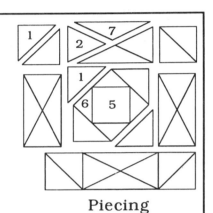

Piecing

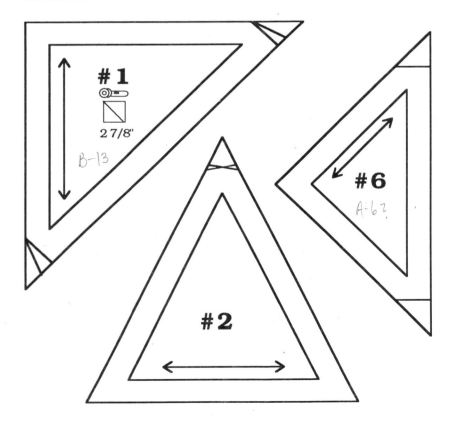

#1
2 7/8"
B-13

#2

#6
A-6?

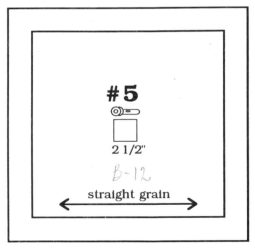

#5
2 1/2"
B-12
straight grain

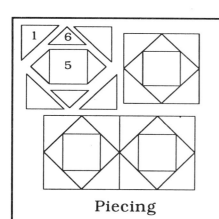

Piecing

This and That

For one block:

Template **#1**: Cut 8 + 8
Template **#5**: Cut 2 + 2
Template **#6**: Cut 16

This and That

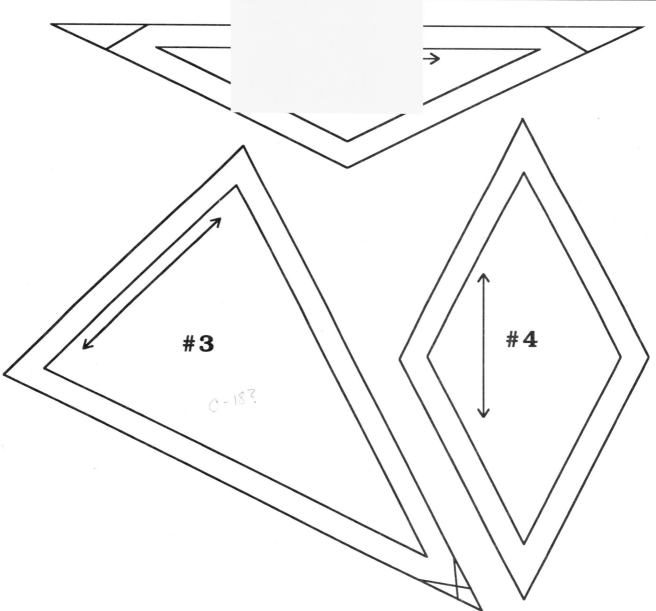

#3

#4

C-18?

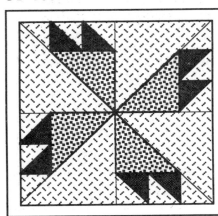

Rosebud

For one block:

Template **#1**: Cut 8 + 12
Template **#2**: Cut 4
Template **#3**: Cut 4

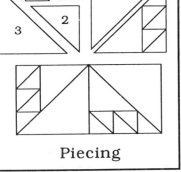

Piecing

Kansas Trouble

For one block:

Template **#3**: Cut 4
Template **#4**: Cut 24 + 16
Template **#5**: Cut 4
Template **#6**: Cut 4

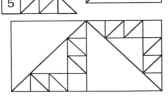

Piecing

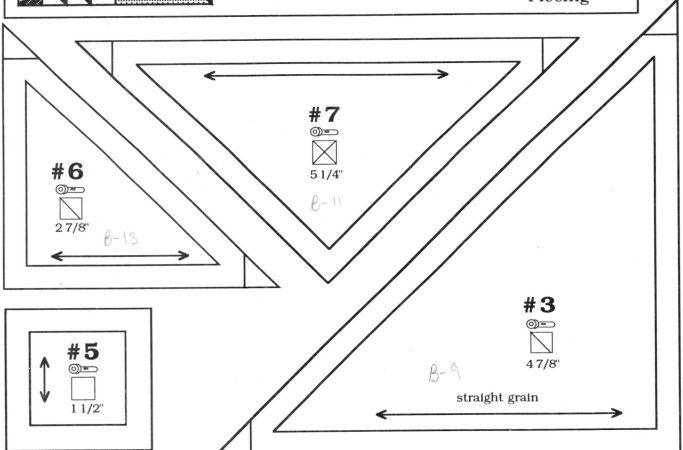

#7

5 1/4"

B-11

#6

2 7/8"

B-13

#3

4 7/8"

B-9

straight grain

#5

1 1/2"

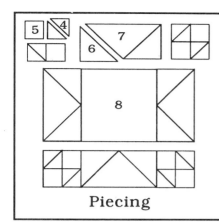

Twinkling Star

For one block:

Template **#4**: Cut 8 + 8
Template **#5**: Cut 8
Template **#6**: Cut 8
Template **#7**: Cut 4
Template **#8**: Cut 1

Piecing

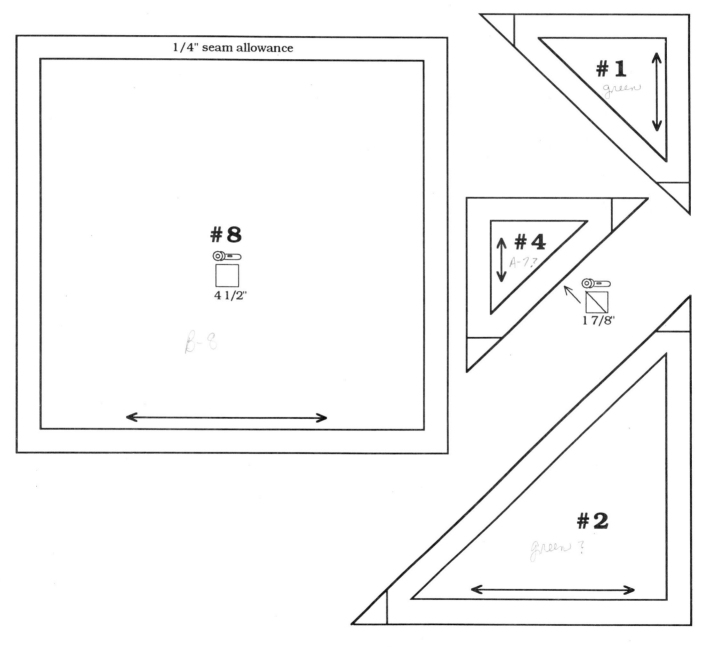

1/4" seam allowance

#8

4 1/2"

#1
green

#4
A-7.?

1 7/8"

#2
green ?

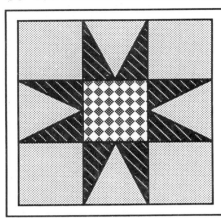

Unknown Star

For one block:

Template **#1**: Cut 4 + 1
Template **#2**: Cut 4
Template **#3**: Cut 4R4

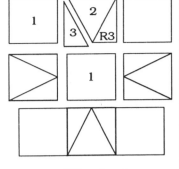

Piecing

Fifty-Four Forty

For one block:

Template **#2**: Cut 4
Template **#3**: Cut 4R4
Template **#4**: Cut 6 + 6 + 8

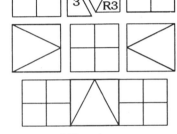

Piecing

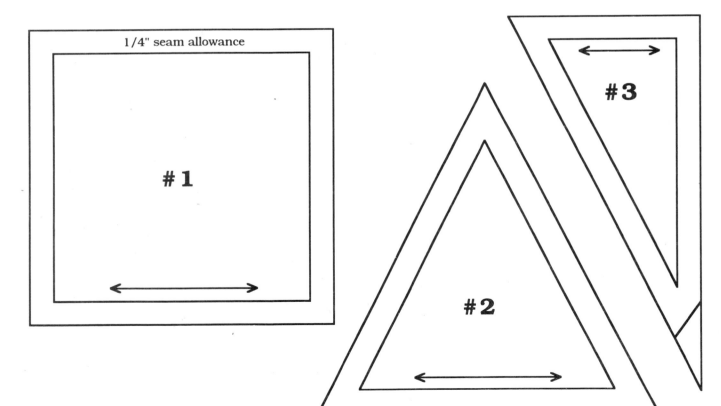

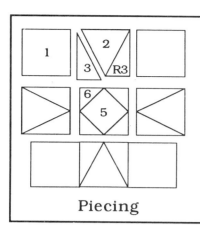

Darting Minnows

For one block:

Template **#1**: Cut 4
Template **#2**: Cut 4
Template **#3**: Cut 4R4
Template **#5**: Cut 1
Template **#6**: Cut 4

Piecing

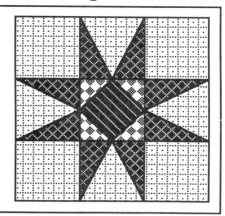

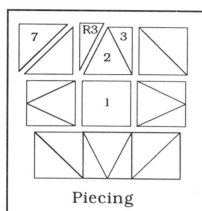

Thistle

For one block:

Template **#1**: Cut 1
Template **#2**: Cut 4
Template **#3**: Cut 4R4
Template **#7**: Cut 4 + 4

Piecing

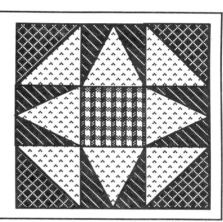

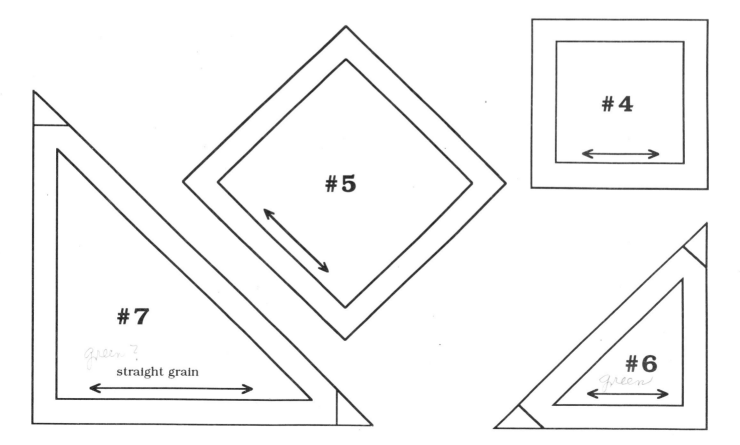

#7

green?

straight grain

#5

#4

#6

green

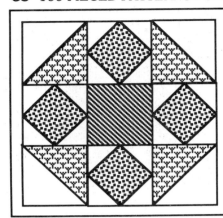

Sawtooth

For one block:

Template **#1**: Cut 1
Template **#3**: Cut 4 + 4
Template **#5**: Cut 4
Template **#6**: Cut 16

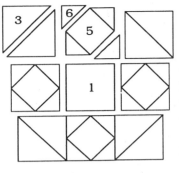

Piecing

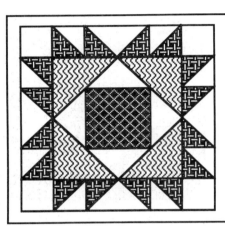

Union Square

For one block:

Template **#1**: Cut 1
Template **#2**: Cut 8
Template **#3**: Cut 4
Template **#4**: Cut 4
Template **#6**: Cut 8 + 16

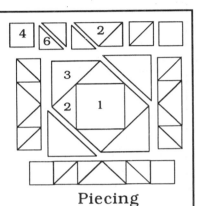

Piecing

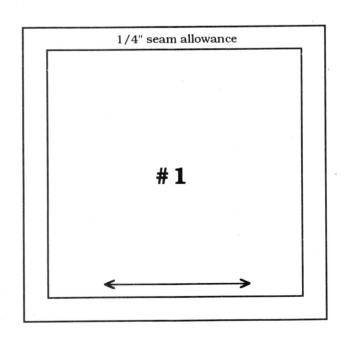

1/4" seam allowance

#1

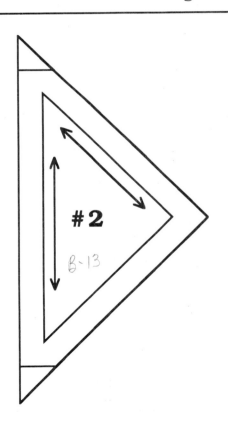

#2

B-13

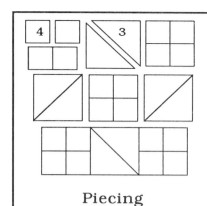

Piecing

Waterwheel

For one block:

Template **#3**: Cut 4 + 4
Template **#4**: Cut 10 + 10

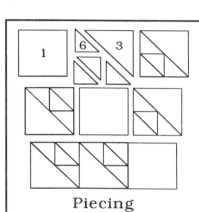

Piecing

Cat's Cradle

For one block:

Template **#1**: Cut 3
Template **#3**: Cut 6
Template **#6**: Cut 18 + 6

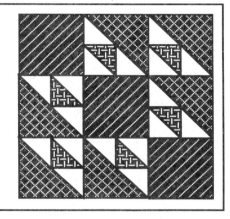

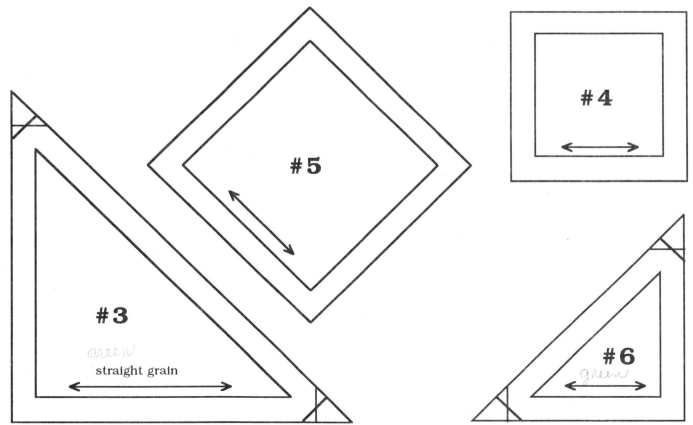

#3

green
straight grain

#5

#4

#6

green

Berkeley

For one block:

Template **#1**: Cut 1
Template **#2**: Cut 4
Template **#3**: Cut 4
Template **#6**: Cut 12
Template **#7**: Cut 4

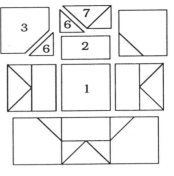

Piecing

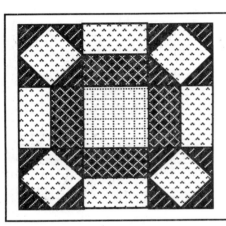

Rolling Stone

For one block:

Template **#1**: Cut 1
Template **#2**: Cut 4 + 4
Template **#5**: Cut 4
Template **#6**: Cut 16

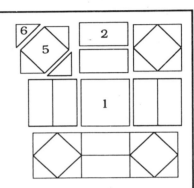

Piecing

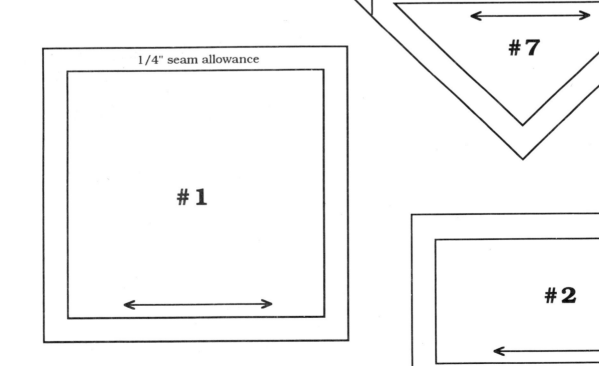

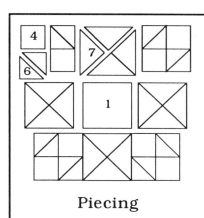

King David's Crown

For one block:

Template **#1**: Cut 1
Template **#4**: Cut 4 + 4
Template **#6**: Cut 8 + 8
Template **#7**: Cut 8 + 8

Piecing

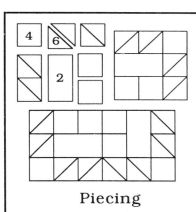

One More Block

For one block:

Template **#2**: Cut 2 + 2
Template **#4**: Cut 6 + 6
Template **#6**: Cut 16 + 16

Piecing

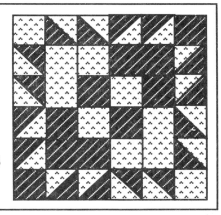

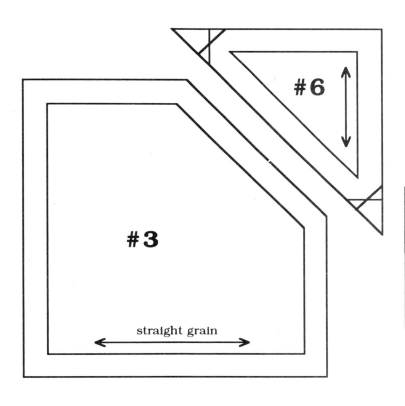

#6

#3

straight grain

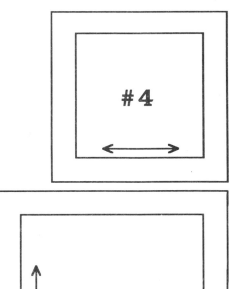

#4

#5

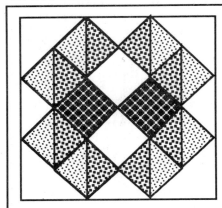

Winter Wheat

For one block:

Template **#1**: Cut 4
Template **#2**: Cut 8 + 8 + 4
Template **#3**: Cut 2 + 2

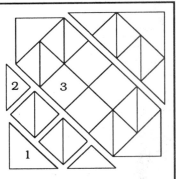

Piecing

Eliza's Ninepatch

For one block:

Template **#2**: Cut 8 + 4
Template **#4**: Cut 4
Template **#5**: Cut 4 + 5

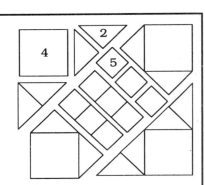

Piecing

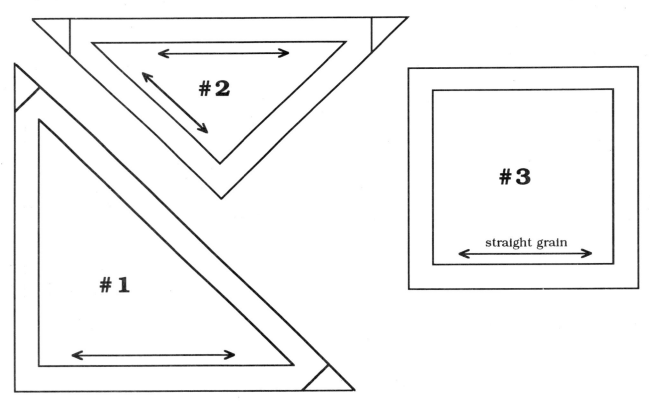

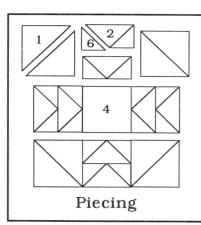

Piecing

Capital "T"

For one block:

Template **#1**: Cut 4 + 4
Template **#2**: Cut 8
Template **#4**: Cut 1
Template **#6**: Cut 16

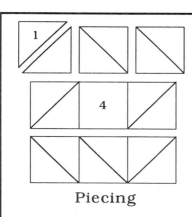

Piecing

Perpetual Motion

For one block:

Template **#1**: Cut 8 + 4 + 4
Template **#4**: Cut 1

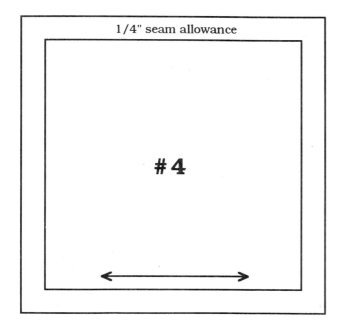

1/4" seam allowance

#4

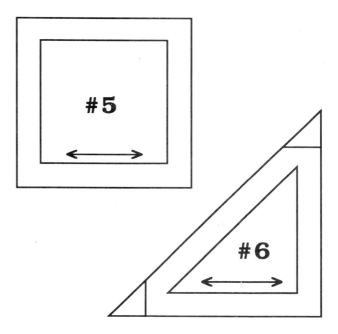

#5

#6

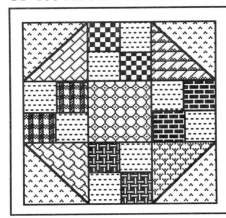

Prairie Queen

For one block:

Template **#1**: Cut 1
Template **#2**: Cut 4 + 4
Template **#3**: Cut 8 + 8

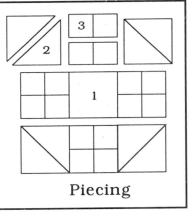

Piecing

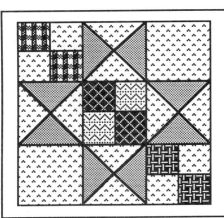

Star Stairway

For one block:

Template **#1**: Cut 2
Template **#3**: Cut 6 + 6
Template **#4**: Cut 8 + 8

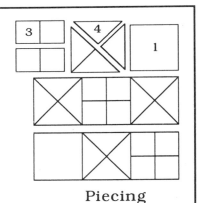

Piecing

Single Irish Chain

For one block:

Template **#1**: Cut 1 + 4
Template **#3**: Cut 8 + 8

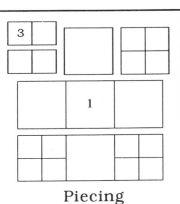

Piecing

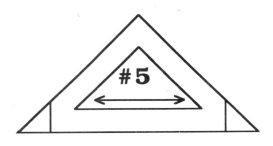

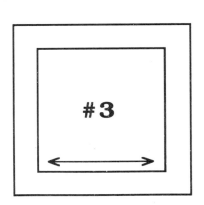

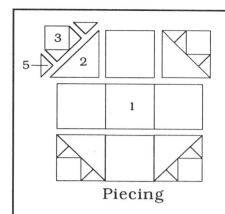

Turkey Tracks

For one block:

Template **#1**: Cut 1 + 4
Template **#2**: Cut 4
Template **#3**: Cut 4
Template **#5**: Cut 8 + 8

Piecing

Jacob's Ladder

For one block:

Template **#2**: Cut 4 + 4
Template **#3**: Cut 10 + 10

Piecing

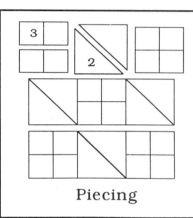

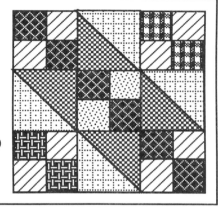

#4

green

#2

straight grain

1/4" seam allowance

#1

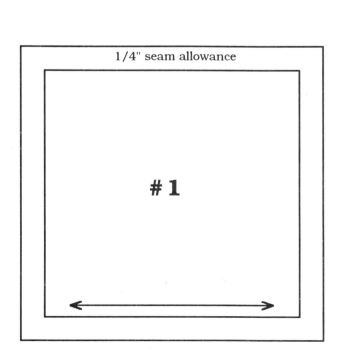

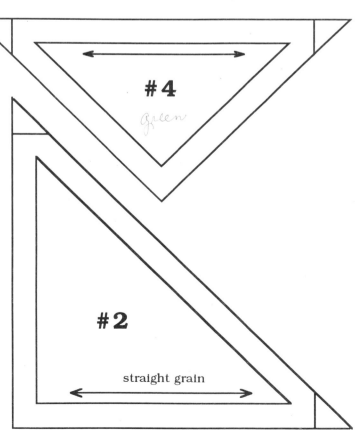

Weathervane

For one block:

Template **#1**: Cut 1
Template **#4**: Cut 4
Template **#5**: Cut 8 + 16
Template **#6**: Cut 4 + 4

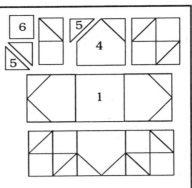

Piecing

Gentleman's Fancy

For one block:

Template **#1**: Cut 1
Template **#2**: Cut 8 + 8
Template **#3**: Cut 4 + 4

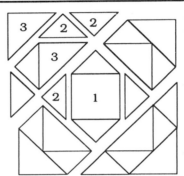

Piecing

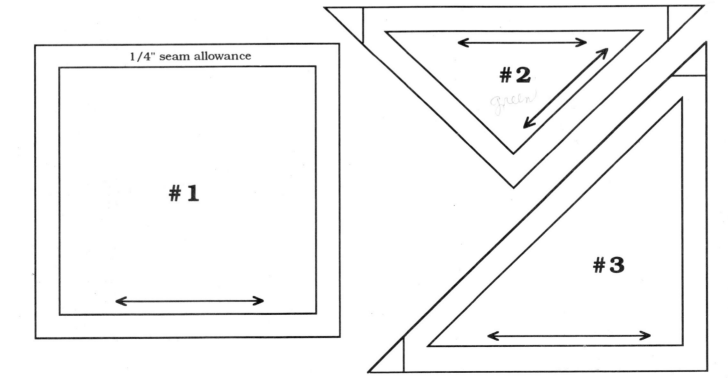

1/4" seam allowance

#1

#2

green

#3

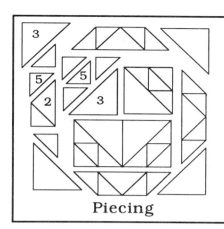

Corn and Beans

For one block:

Template **#2**: Cut 4
Template **#3**: Cut 4 + 2 + 2
Template **#5**: Cut 12 + 20

Piecing

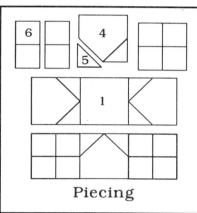

Stairway to the Stars

For one block:

Template **#1**: Cut 1
Template **#4**: Cut 4
Template **#5**: Cut 8
Template **#6**: Cut 8 + 8

Piecing

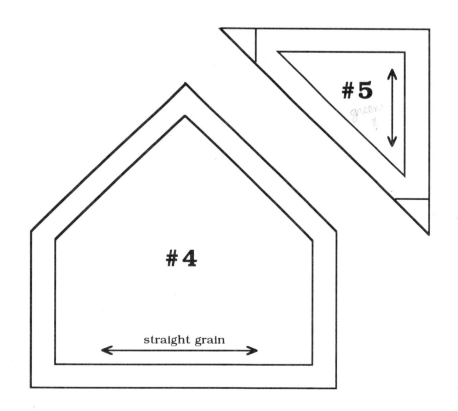

#5

green

#4

straight grain

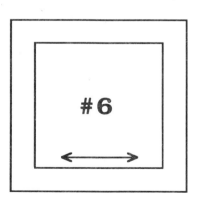

#6

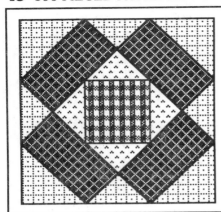

Nonsense

For one block:

Template **#1**: Cut 4
Template **#2**: Cut 4 + 4
Template **#3**: Cut 1
Template **#4**: Cut 4

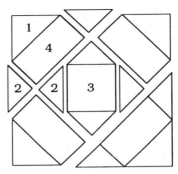

Piecing

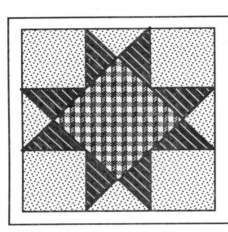

Variable Star II

For one block:

Template **#2**: Cut 8 + 4
Template **#3**: Cut 4
Template **#5**: Cut 1

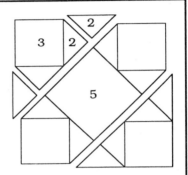

Piecing

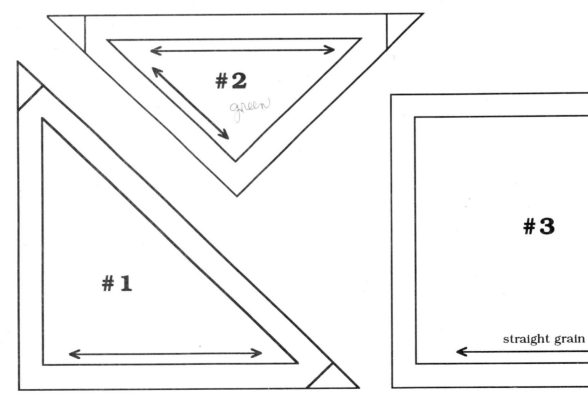

#2

green

#1

#3

straight grain

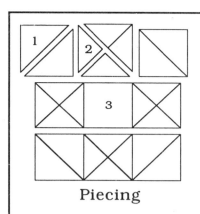

Piecing

Swamp Patch

For one block:

Template **#1**: Cut 4 + 4
Template **#2**: Cut 8 + 8
Template **#3**: Cut 1

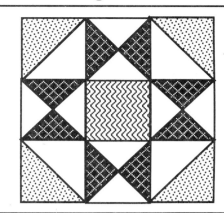

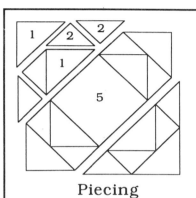

Piecing

Diversion

For one block:

Template **#1**: Cut 4 + 4
Template **#2**: Cut 4 + 8
Template **#5**: Cut 1

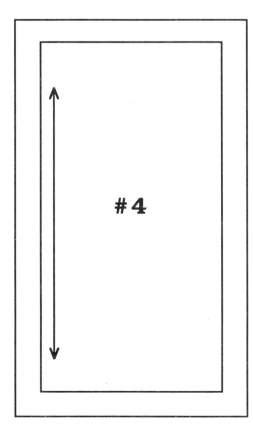

#4

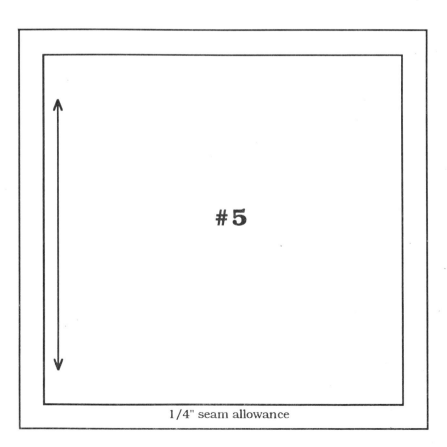

#5

1/4" seam allowance

Italian Tile

For one block:

Template **#1**: Cut 4 + 4
Template **#2**: Cut 4
Template **#3**: Cut 8 + 24

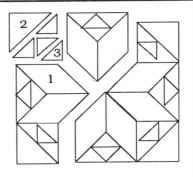

Piecing

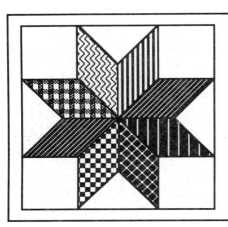

Le Moyne Star

For one block:

Template **#1**: Cut 8
Template **#2**: Cut 4
Template **#7**: Cut 4

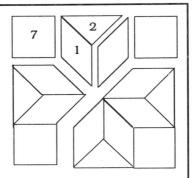

Piecing

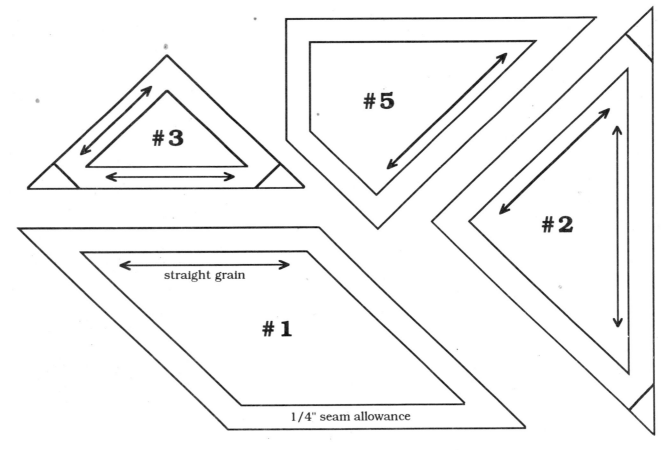

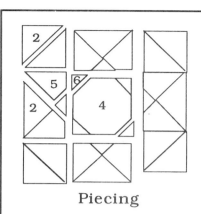

Quiet Time

For one block:

Template **#2**: Cut 4 + 8
Template **#4**: Cut 1
Template **#5**: Cut 8
Template **#6**: Cut 8

Piecing

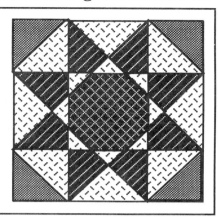

Twisting Star

For one block:

Template **#2**: Cut 4 + 4 + 4
Template **#4**: Cut 1
Template **#7**: Cut 4

Piecing

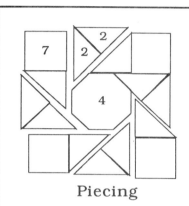

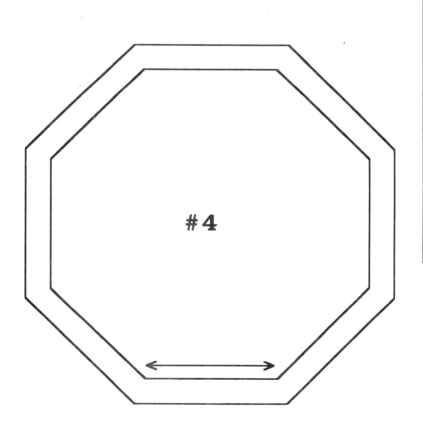

#4

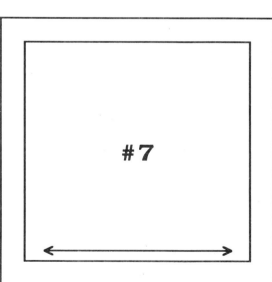

#7

#6

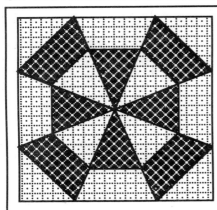

Spider's Web

For one block:

Template **#1**: Cut 4
Template **#2**: Cut 4 + 4
Template **#3**: Cut 4 + 4

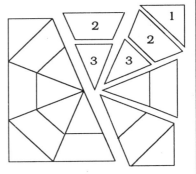

Piecing

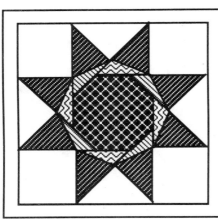

Ringed Star

For one block:

Template **#1**: Cut 4
Template **#4**: Cut 4
Template **#5**: Cut 1
Template **#6**: Cut 8
Template **#9**: Cut 8

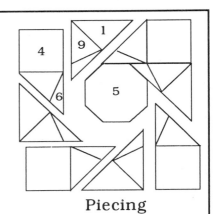

Piecing

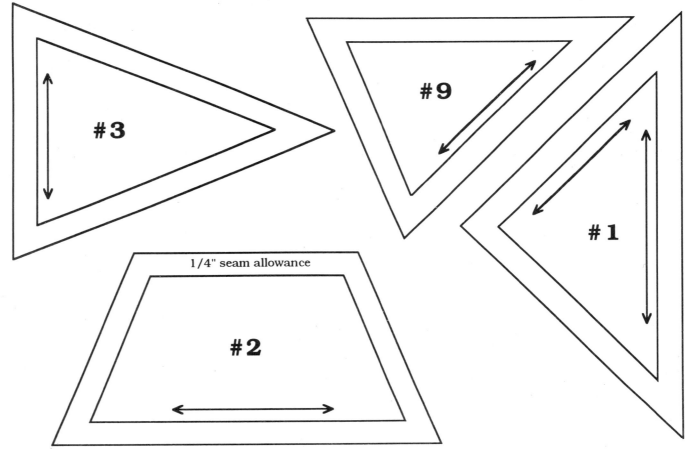

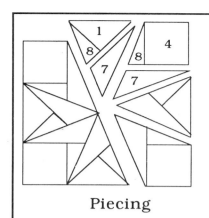

Piecing

Twirling Star

For one block:

Template **#1**: Cut 4
Template **#4**: Cut 4
Template **#7**: Cut 4 + 4
Template **#8**: Cut 8

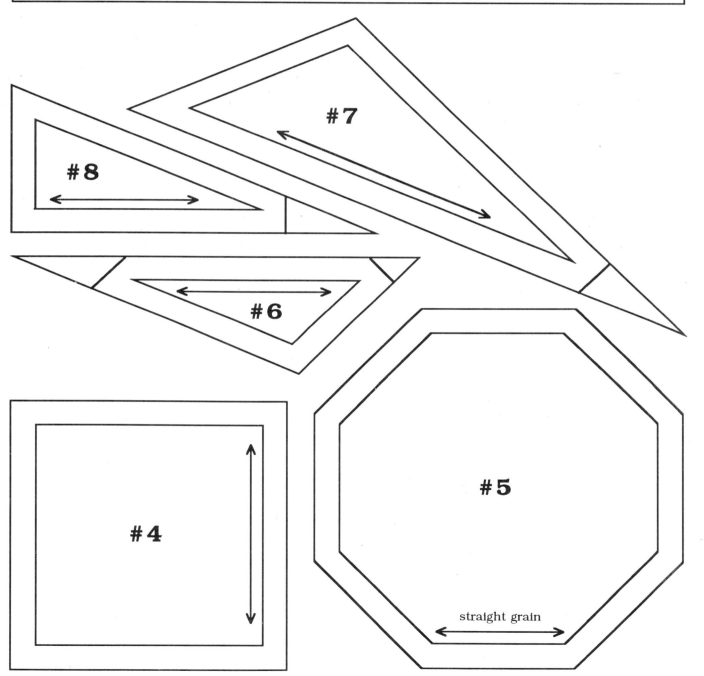

#7

#8

#6

#4

#5

straight grain

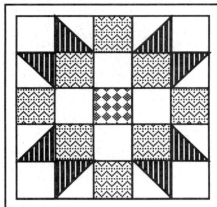

Sister's Choice

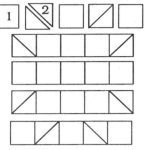

Piecing

For one block:

Template **#1**: Cut 8 + 9
Template **#2**: Cut 8 + 8

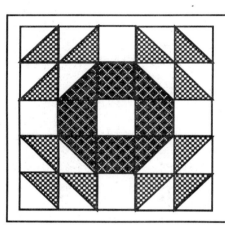

Wedding Ring

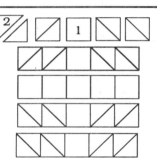

Piecing

For one block:

Template **#1**: Cut 4 + 5
Template **#2**: Cut 4 + 12 + 16

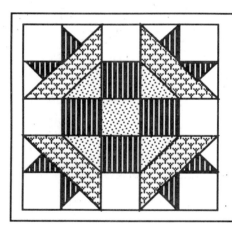

David and Goliath

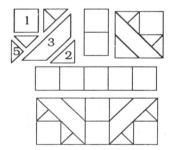

For one block:

Template **#1**: Cut 1 + 4 + 8
Template **#2**: Cut 4
Template **#3**: Cut 4
Template **#5**: Cut 8 + 8

Piecing

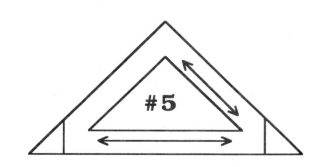

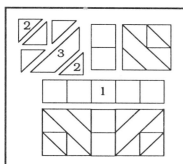

Red Cross

For one block:

Template **#1**: Cut 1 + 4 + 4
Template **#2**: Cut 4 + 4 + 12
Template **#3**: Cut 4

Piecing

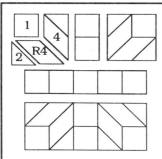

Farmer's Daughter

For one block:

Template **#1**: Cut 1 + 4 + 8
Template **#2**: Cut 8
Template **#4**: Cut 4 + R4

Piecing

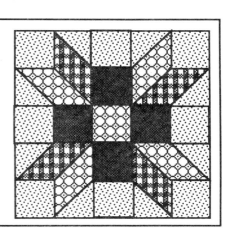

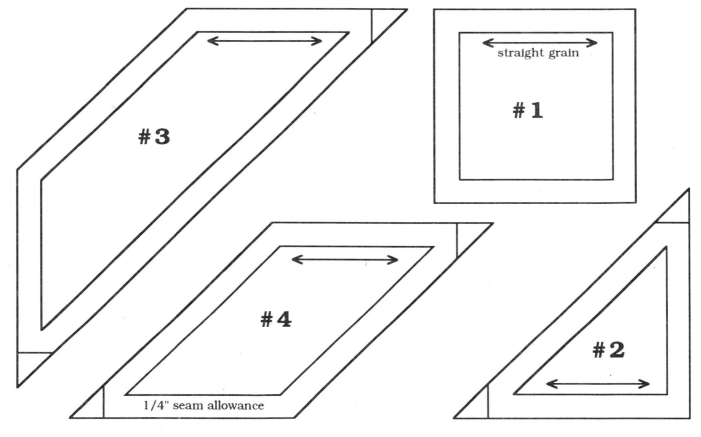

#3

#1

straight grain

#4

1/4" seam allowance

#2

Mexican Rose

For one block:

Template **#1**: Cut 1 + 4
Template **#2**: Cut 4
Template **#4**: Cut 4
Template **#5**: Cut 4
Template **#6**: Cut 8 + 8

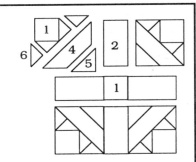

Piecing

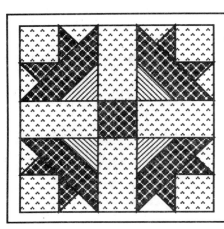

Duck Paddle

For one block:

Template **#1**: Cut 1 + 4
Template **#2**: Cut 4
Template **#4**: Cut 4
Template **#5**: Cut 4
Template **#6**: Cut 8 + 8

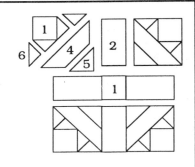

Piecing

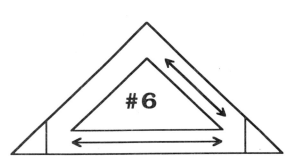

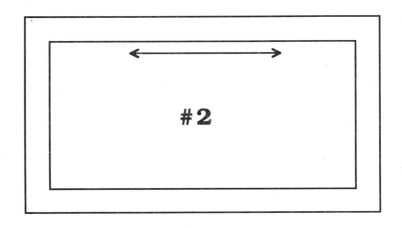

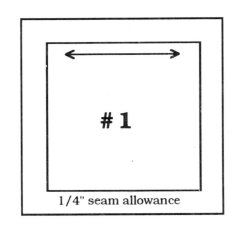

1/4" seam allowance

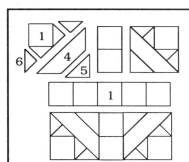

Piecing

Hands All Around

For one block:

Template **#1**: Cut 4 + 9
Template **#4**: Cut 4
Template **#5**: Cut 4
Template **#6**: Cut 8 + 8

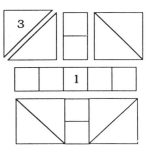

Piecing

Churn Dash

For one block:

Template **#1**: Cut 1 + 4 + 4
Template **#3**: Cut 4 + 4

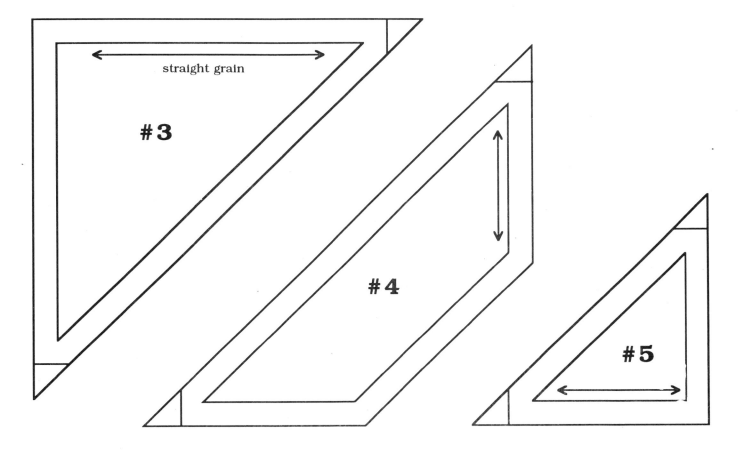

straight grain

#3

#4

#5

Quality

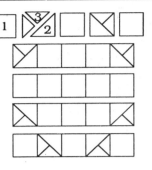

For one block:

Template **#1**: Cut 4 + 13
Template **#2**: Cut 8
Template **#3**: Cut 8 + 8

Piecing

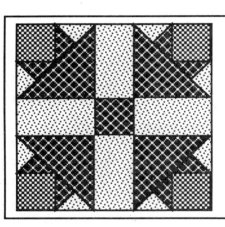

Goose Tracks

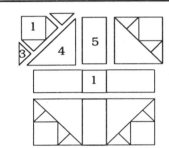

For one block:

Template **#1**: Cut 1 + 4
Template **#3**: Cut 8 + 8
Template **#4**: Cut 4
Template **#5**: Cut 4

Piecing

Ducks and Duckings

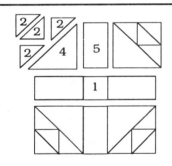

For one block:

Template **#1**: Cut 1
Template **#2**: Cut 4 + 12
Template **#4**: Cut 4
Template **#5**: Cut 4

Piecing

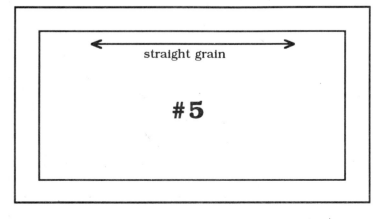

straight grain

#5

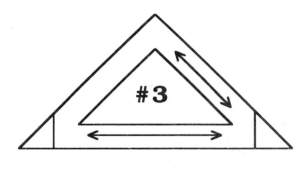

#3

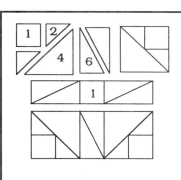

Crazy Anne

For one block:

Template **#1**: Cut 1 + 4
Template **#2**: Cut 8
Template **#4**: Cut 4
Template **#6**: Cut 4 + 4

Piecing

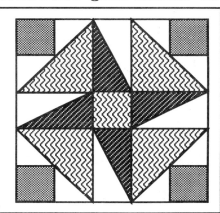

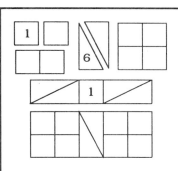

Tiny Dancer

For one block:

Template **#1**: Cut 4 + 5 + 8
Template **#6**: Cut 4 + 4

Piecing

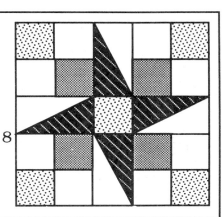

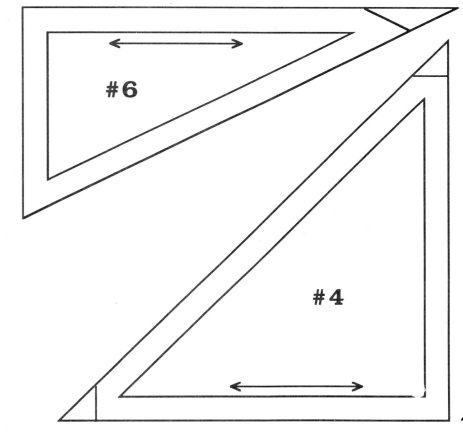

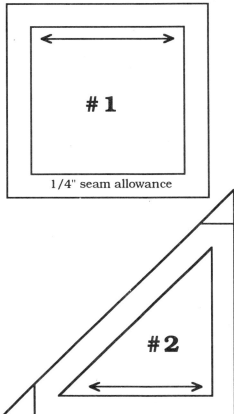

#6

#4

#2

#1

1/4" seam allowance

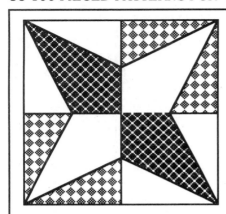

Candlelight

For one block:

Template **#1**: Cut 2R2 + 2R2
Template **#4**: Cut 2 + 2

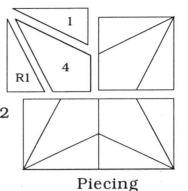

Piecing

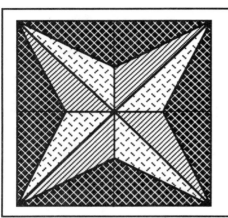

Job's Troubles

For one block:

Template **#1**: Cut 4R4
Template **#4**: Cut 4 (Sew 2 1/2" wide bias strips together. Press seams to one side. Place #4 template point to point on seam line; cut two-triangle shapes as one piece.)

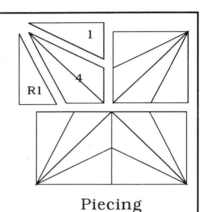

Piecing

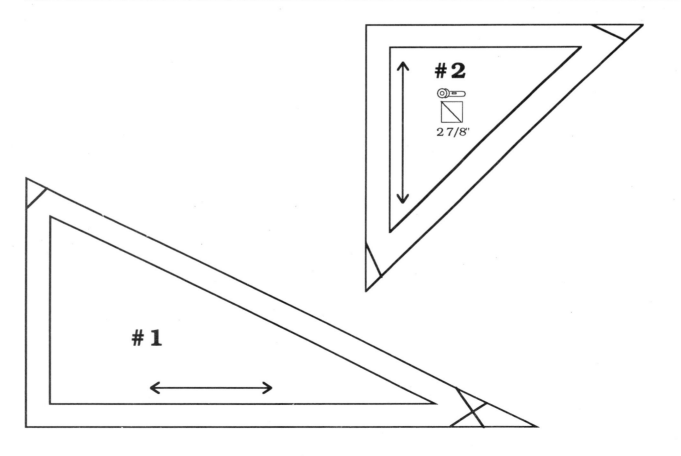

#2

2 7/8"

#1

Kayak

For one block:

Template **#1**: Cut 2R2 + 2R2

Template **#2**: Cut 2 + 2

Template **#3**: Cut 2 + 2

Piecing

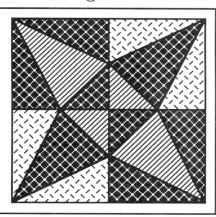

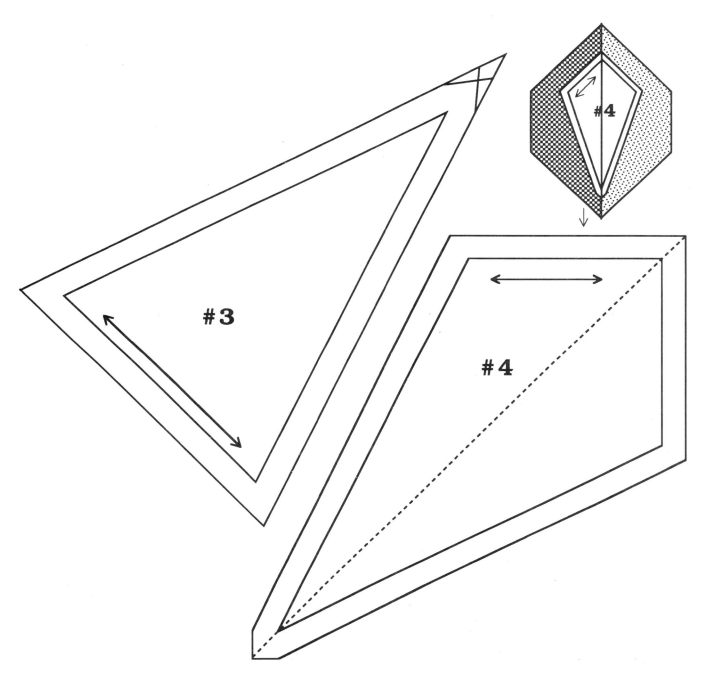

#3

#4

#4

Blazing Star

For one block:

Template **#1**: Cut 4R4
Template **#2**: Cut 4 + R4
Template **#3**: Cut 4 + R4

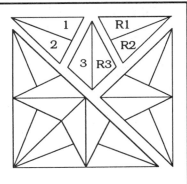

Piecing

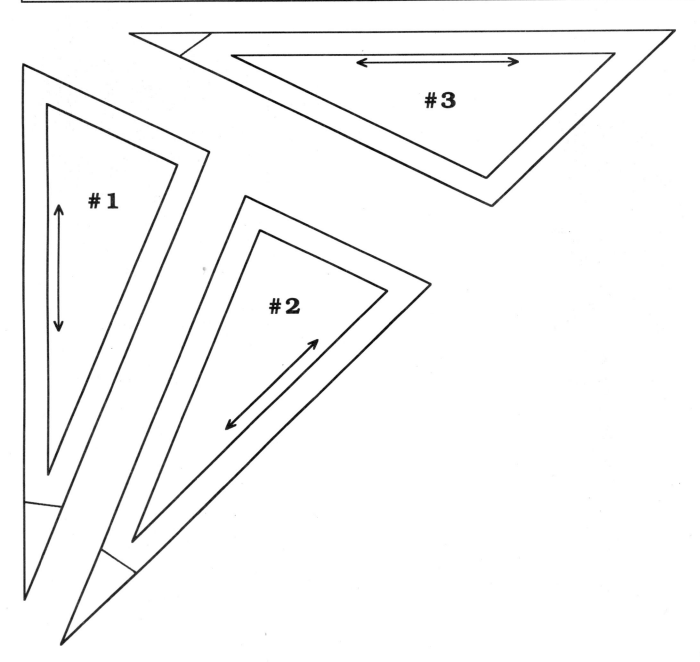

DIMENSIONS: 58" x 74"

MATERIALS: 44"-wide Fabric

2 yards total assorted navy prints (8 different fat quarters) for block piecing   *10*

3 yards total assorted light prints --"white-with navy" (12 different fat quarters) for block piecing   *16*

1 yard total assorted butterscotch prints (4 *8* different fat quarters) for block piecing

2 yards navy print for border and for binding

Backing: 3 1/2 yards
Batting and thread to finish

QUILT PARTS

Assorted pieced blocks, 8"
Make 18

Chimneys and Cornerstones, 8" alternate blocks
Make 17

Chimneys and Cornerstones half-block, 4" x 8"
Make 14

Log Cabin half-block, 4" x 8"
Make 10

Log Cabin corner block, 4"
Make 4

SAMPLER QUILT

DIRECTIONS

1. First choose, then cut and piece 18 different **8" blocks** from pages 9-62. You may use the same designs I chose, or try different ones. Reading right to left, the blocks in the quilt pictured on the inside back cover are as follows:
    1. Variable Star, p. 13
    2. Ducks and Ducklings, p. 58
    3. Blazing Star, p. 62
    4. Centennial. p. 11
    5. Ringed Star, p. 52
    6. Capital "T", p. 43
    7. Twisting Star, p. 51
    8. Crazy Anne, p. 59
    9. Twirling Star, p. 53
    10. Rising Star, p. 10
    11. Jack in the Pulpit, p. 10
    12. Judy's Star, p. 12
    13. Rambler, p. 12
    14. Spider's Web, p. 52
    15. Goose Tracks, p. 58
    16. Grandmother's Favorite, p.15
    17. Dutchman's Puzzle, p. 11
    18. Hovering Hawks, p. 26

2. Cut* and piece 17 **Chimneys and Corner-stones alternate blocks** according to the pattern found on page 22. Cut Template #1 from butterscotch fabric; Template #2 from navy; and Templates #3, #4 and #5 from assorted lights.

3. Cut and piece 14 **Chimneys and Cornerstones half-blocks**. Use templates #2, #3, #4, #5 found on pages 22-23 and #11 on page 64.
For one Chimneys and Cornerstones half block, 4" x 8":
    Template #2: Cut 6 navy + 2 light
    Template #3: Cut 1 butterscotch + 3 light
    Template #4: Cut 1 light
    Template #5: Cut 1 light
    Template #11: Cut 2 light

Piecing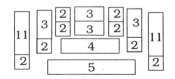

**Cutting Tip: Rotary cut strips of assorted light fabrics 1 1/2" wide; then subcut them to appropriate lengths.*

4. Cut and piece 10 **Log Cabin half-blocks**.
Use templates #3, #4 and #5 found on pages
22-23 and #11 on this page.
For one Log Cabin half block, 4" x 8":
   Template #3: Cut 4 light
   Template #4: Cut 3 light
   Template #5: Cut 1 light
   Template #11: Cut 2 light

Piecing

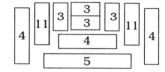

5. Cut and piece 4 **Log Cabin corner blocks**.
Use templates #2 and #3 found on pages 22-
23 and #11 on this page.
For one Log Cabin corner block, 4" x 4":
   Template #2: Cut 2 light
   Template #3: Cut 2 light
   Template #4: Cut 1 light
   Template #11: Cut 2 light

Piecing

6. Set 8" sampler blocks, Chimneys and Cornerstones alternate blocks, Log Cabin half-
blocks and Log Cabin corner blocks together
in rows. Sew rows together. Press for
opposing seams.

7. From navy border print, cut 4 strips 5"
wide from the lengthwise grain for borders.
Add side borders first, then top and bottom
trimming extra length as necessary. Use
blunt sewn corners.

8. Add batting and backing. Quilt.

9. From remaining navy border print, cut
9 1/4 yards of 1 1/2"-wide bias strips for
binding. Bind quilt edges.

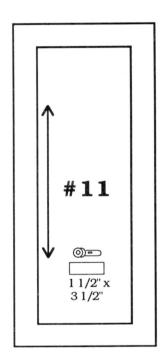

#11

1 1/2" x
3 1/2"